DEVELOP A
GENIUS
MINDSET

UNLEASH YOUR FULL POTENTIAL
AND ACHIEVE UNIMAGINABLE SUCCESS

DEVELOP A
GENIUS
MINDSET

UNLEASH YOUR FULL POTENTIAL
AND ACHIEVE UNIMAGINABLE SUCCESS

J.R. FITZGERALD

Printed in the United States of America

First Printing Edition.
1 3 5 7 9 11 13 15 17 19 21

A Purist Publishing Production

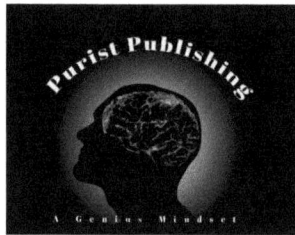

A Genius Mindset Book®

The International Standard Book Number (ISBN)
for each format is located below:
Title: DEVELOP A GENIUS MINDSET

This title is available in paperback or in digital format:
Look for it in Audiobook Creation Exchange (ACX) format, soon:

PAPERBACK: (ISBN) 978-1-953951-01-4
EBOOK: (ISBN) 978-1-953951-00-7
Published by Purist Publishing
Houston, Texas

For my smart, persistent, and beloved son,
whom I love more then the air I breathe.
And much appreciation, love, and gratitude
to my mother, for without you, your sacrifice,
your strength, and your compassion, none
of this would have been possible.
Thank you.

CONTENTS

PREFACE

Thank you for choosing this book: *Develop A Genius Mindset*. We are not born geniuses, so we must learn all that we can to become one. My mission is to encourage those who want to learn, study, and empower themselves in all aspects of their lives. This book's main objective is to introduce to you, what I believe to be, the fundamental principles that can help you live a more successful, prosperous, purposeful, and meaningful life.

In a fast-paced changing world, I needed to change strategically, technically, personally, positively, and professionally. But before I could grow financially, personally, and professionally, I needed to change my physical state, but more importantly, my mental state of mind. So, I disciplined myself to read the necessary books or listen to audiobooks at home, while exercising, and even while I drove to and from work and the university. I watched specific seminars, read and watched many important mini-lessons in my area of interest, and I changed my daily habits to focus only on the best success principles to reprogram my mind for ultimate success. I began to condition my mind, something I had never done in all my life. I experienced positive results immediately.

The fundamental principles you will read within this text, helped me develop intimately, personally, spiritually, and professionally. At the beginning of my journey to create success in all aspects of my life, during the research, during the writing process, and as I continued to attend classes at the University of Houston, I disciplined myself so I could develop and discover my true purpose in life. It all began by setting goals for myself, writing them down, and taking action on those goals every day. Writing down my goals and revisiting them on a daily and weekly basis changed my life instantly. I created a roadmap, a blueprint for my future, and now, opportunities, possibilities, and personal and professional communication is intentional not accidental.

We all want to succeed in life. We all are chasing some sort of wealth and prosperity. I wanted to succeed in all aspects of my life, to take care of my family, to actually set goals and accomplish them. My mission is to relay a positive, informative, and a constructive message. My job is to not only inspire and motivate but to acknowledge that you to have the ability to change the course of your life. While we may not always have the ability to change our current destination or location, but we do have the capability to change our way of thinking and change the way we look at things. Someone once said, "If you change the way you look at things, the things you look at will change." Positive change is possible in any business industry and during any crisis, and during any time of the year: in warm weather, cold weather, raining or snowing. You have the power.

My mission is to let you know that success is possible. My mission is to help others see and realize and bring out their full potential in the process of my self-development. My satisfaction is helping others by providing them with the vital information that can transform their lives–the exact information and the fundamental principles, disciplines, and the philosophy that transformed my life.

During my many years of research and throughout the process of writing this book, I gained more knowledge, more insights, more inspiration, motivation, dedication, and admiration for what I believe to be the fundamental principles for success. They are: setting goals, having a mission, being selfish, being responsible, taking risks, facing adversities, creating courage, having high expectations, exercising your mind, failing and succeeding, the importance of first impressions, visualizing your success, self-education, maintaining a rich mindset, knowing that success leaves clues, self-discipline, self-confidence, communication skills, time management, and your overall personal development. There may be more or there may be fewer, but these basic principles are the mastery and the fundamentals that continue to help me live a happier life, a more meaningful life, and a richer and successful life.

Under any circumstances, I continue to study, educate, and practice every single principle in this book. These personal development skills, techniques, and strategies have helped me condition my mind, as well as, help me focus and strengthen my self-esteem. Overall, I believe every person has the ability to grow and stretch themselves physically and mentally.

While reading this book, incorporate the significant principles for your success that you find appealing to you. Execute these principles, change your mindset and experience the life-changing skills that can help you take your potential to the next level, meet new people, discover new opportunities, and possibly the ability to communicate globally by all means necessary. Just imagine the possibilities and ideas and endeavors that await you. You deserve it!

I experimented with these principles, techniques, and strategies and they can work for you—immediately! If, you will put in the time, effort, and discipline yourself to change your life; only then, will you reap the benefits of your success that you seek in all aspects of your life. Double your income, network, become more knowledgeable, gain more opportunities, and gain the self-confidence to walk through doors that can help you meet new people and become more successful than your ever thought was possible. Why? Because success is possible!

Over time, during the writing process of this book, I recharged my life, reprogrammed my mind, and yes, success is possible! I discovered a powerful vision that had been within me all along. I saw things more clearly. My mindset changed. My passion and purpose increased, my goals, which had never been written down, became a reality. I truly believe I resurrected the essential keys for my ongoing success that had been stored in my mind all along. You can do it too.

To the Reader: My mission is to help you, the reader, the entrepreneur, the knowledge seeker, the future leader, whomever you may be, to help you unlock your success, unlock your creativity and full potential—one chapter at a time, one day at a time, or however long it takes you to realize the greatness within you. It is a fact; no scientist has ever discovered the limit of human potential. We have greatness within us. Our minds are our biggest asset and we are capable of learning and solving problems, our mind can get us what we want, and the beauty is, we just have to gain the courage and knowledge to change our lives, control it, and get out of our comfort zone to achieve the success we desire, gain the attention we desire, and gain the financial freedom we desire.

After many years of research, thousands of hours of studying, and many trials and errors, I now provide you with the fundamental skills, techniques, strategies, and concepts that instantly helped me change, grow, and turn my life around for the better. If I can do it; you can do it, we all can do it! Do not wish for success, create success by gaining the necessary skills and knowledge that can guide you.

As I changed my life, I learned and continued to study and *Develop A Genius Mindset*—to develop, balance, believe, structure, accomplish, and master my mind, my life, and to chase, conquer, and fulfill my dreams and my goals in my own life. Every skill is learnable, so do not be discouraged. You too can learn the necessary skills in your field of interest that can transform you and your future.

Also, during the process of creating and writing this book, what I believe to be a self-reflection of my life, I discovered and designed a simple system—a system of the sciences of emotions, thoughts, decisions, and actions that encapsulate each fundamental principle in each chapter of this book. My theory is, our emotions affect our thoughts, our thoughts affect our decisions, and our decisions affect our actions. In the real world, our actions define our results in all aspects of our lives. In every chapter, I have broken down each theoretical point as a subheading in each chapter, so there will be an introduction to the chapter, four subheadings: your emotions, your thoughts, your decisions, and your actions, and a summary and execution box in that order. The chapters are intuitive, direct, and simple to read. Read, study, and practice every principle in this book at your convenience. When you are willing and ready to do so, unleash the power and the full potential within you. Read one chapter a day or read the whole book in a day.

If you want to recharge your life and add more knowledge into your mental factory, change your current situation or you just want to enhance your personal development and the fabric of your life, this book is for you. Remember, if you learn more, want more, see more, and read more, you will earn more in a lifetime than you ever thought was possible. Take charge of your life; take charge and leap toward your success, today! Read this book in its entirety and *Develop A Genius Mindset*, today. Thank you.

-J.R. Fitzgerald

ACKNOWLEDGMENTS

This piece of work and to Develop A Genius Mindset would not have been possible had it not been for the following individuals, their content, their words of wisdom, their knowledge and professionalism, and while some of these contributors are no longer alive, their message and their legacy lives on, metaphorically speaking.

Thank you: Aristotle, Neil Armstrong, Les Brown, Brendon Burchard, Felice Buscaglia, Jack Canfield, Evan Carmichael, Walt Disney, Wayne Dyer, Michael Jordan, Tai Lopez, Steve Maraboli, John C. Maxwell, Earl Nightingale, Dan Pena, Bob Proctor, Mel Robbins, Tony Robbins, Jim Rohn, Brian Tracy, Oprah Winfrey, and Zig Ziglar. Their videos, books and audiobooks, webinars, seminars, lectures, brief talks, and interviews, helped me overcome my fear, dominate my body and mind, but more importantly, helped me begin and complete this writing project. Thank you, everyone.

I would also like to thank everyone that has crossed my path, from friends to family, that have positively encouraged me to pursue my education. In particular, the whole Hernandez family and Juanita, my second mom, for always believing in me. Also, a warm thanks to the Thomas family, especially Chris, for always trusting me. A big thanks to my grandmother for reminding me to slow down and focus; she also taught me how to plant trees, flowers, and enjoy the outdoors.

Also, thank you to everyone at Lone Star College-University Park, from the students to faculty and staff, but more importantly, one of my mentors, Ardalan Shah, whose words of wisdom and leadership, guided me, inspired me, and pushed me to succeed in all aspects of my life. Thank you.

Likewise, I would like to thank the University of Houston, its students, faculty and staff, I encountered many diverse individuals with many interesting stories that captivated me and moved me, touched me, and inspired me. Thank you.

Finally, I would like to thank my son, whom I love more than the air I breathe, you changed me. But the number one person in my life that has sacrificed her physical and mental health to help me, was my mother, Blanca Esthella Pena De Rodriguez. This book would not have been completed had it not been for you. I love you, mom, and thank you for all that you have done for me. I am a U.S. citizen because of you, and I am even more grateful for that. Thank you, everyone.

Sincerely and Yours truly,
J.R. Fitzgerald

INTRODUCTION

Within the text of this book, you will learn the fundamental principles for success and why it is important to *Develop A Genius Mindset*. You will learn the importance of being goal-oriented, identifying a mission in your life, learn the art of gratitude and gain a positive attitude, the importance of taking responsibilities for your actions, and the importance of taking a risk in your own life that can transform you and your life.

You will also be introduced to the importance of embracing adversities in your life, bringing out the courage from within you, creating high expectations in your life that can turn your life around for the better. Not to mention, you will understand that by replacing bad habits with positive, life-changing habits—habits that high-performers, entrepreneurs, and high-achievers all over the world have used for decades, can and will create success in all aspects of your life. If they can do it, and I can do it; then, you can do it. We all can do it! Living a more successful life is possible. We just have to take positive action, today, tomorrow, and every day.

You will also learn that you do not need to reinvent success, for everything you need for living a more purposeful and meaningful life has been written, recorded, and implemented and modeled in some form or way: through media, through seminars, conferences, books, audiobooks, e-books, articles, and videos, just to name a few. You name it; the resources you need are available; you just have to become resourceful. Remember, every skill is learnable.

You will learn the fundamental principles, techniques, and strategies to reach your full potential and *Develop A Genius Mindset*. Do you want to turn your life around? It is possible! Do you want to earn more money? It is possible. Do you want to meet more prospects? It is possible. Do you want to gain influence and become a stronger leader and gain more followers? It is possible. Never give up on your dreams!

As you read, you will also learn why it is important to exercise physically and mentally; the importance of experimenting, failing, and getting back up and succeeding in your life and why first impressions are important. You will also gain insight and learn about the power of visualization.

As you read and study, you will absorb and learn to appreciate the importance of self-education, how to develop a rich and positive mindset. Also, in this book, you will grasp the concept to not judge others, but instead, to learn from those who have succeeded and failed before you. Many have said, "Success leaves clues." I can attest this. The creation of this book is my evidence.

As you grasp the concepts in this book and *Develop A Genius Mindset*, you will continue to understand the importance of self-discipline, self-confidence, communication, time-management, the importance of finding a mentor; and of course, the art of personal development, which I believe is the #1 fundamental skill that every person should learn if they want to become more successful in all aspects of their life.

As you read and study this book, you will learn the fundamental principles for living a more successful life; you will absorb and appreciate the art of personal fulfillment, personal success, and learn why it is important to *Develop A Genius Mindset*. Thank you and may all your thoughts come into focus. Thank you for taking the time to read this in its entirety and from me to you: *Develop A Genius Mindset*, today, tomorrow and for the future of your family.

Yours truly,
-*J.R. Fitzgerald*

CHAPTER 1

Be Goal-Oriented

An Overview

A person living without a goal is a person living without any expectations for their future. You must set small and large goals. You must write down and set short-term and long-term goals. No matter the size of the goal, take time to think, reflect, and imagine your goal already in the progress of fulfillment.

More importantly, take the time to write your goals down within a notepad and keep track of your progress, make a plan to achieve that goal, and take massive action to accomplish that goal. Also, make yourself accountable for your actions. Actions do speak louder than words, especially when you have goals set in place to fulfill. There is no goal to difficult to achieve if you can feel it in your heart—and believe—believe that you can succeed.

1.1 Technique 1: Your Emotions

Every living person feels wonderful, powerful, and important when they complete their goals, even when they are small ones. You are gaining momentum and self-confidence as you complete a new goal. Then another and another, and by the time you know it, achieving your goals will become a habit, and you will become unstoppable. Eventually, we want to repeat the process of feeling confident, achieving daily, and pursuing new goals.

1.2 Technique 2: Your Thoughts

If you can think it or dream it, you can make your goals a reality. The key to succeeding in accomplishing your goals is to remain optimistic, read or review everything there is about your goal. Learn from others who you admire. Or, learn from high-performance people who have clear long-term goals. But more importantly, you must feed your mind with mental protein; read and absorb enriching material; surround yourself with other goal-oriented individuals, and stay away from time wasters and naysayers.

1.3 Technique 3: Your Decisions

Only you can decide to change your mindset. Remain strong and confident, so that you can succeed at completing your goals and reaching your full potential. Everybody has greatness within them. Only a positive decision will change your life from being an average person—to propelling you to become the successful person you are meant to be. Decide to take action, today.

The important thing to know is: You must take action on your goals, now, or one day will pass, and then another, and your goals will never become a reality. Decide to control your own thoughts and your own goals, and you will be unstoppable. Mostly all leaders and high-achievers are goal-oriented individuals. Decide to become a goal-oriented individual, a leadership quality, and change the way you approach new goals, new opportunities, and new innovations in your life.

1.4 Technique 4: Your Actions

Finally, taking action on your goals will ultimately define your future success. Without action, that thought about changing your life, completing a new goal, gaining wealth, and fulfilling your ultimate destiny, whatever it may be, will remain only a figment of your imagination if you do not act on it immediately.

Map out a plan, create a blueprint for your goal because everything we need to accomplish in life needs a map, a plan, an agenda, and some sort of guidance with the end in mind. Take control of your life, today.

Since the beginning of civilization, men and women have taken action to change the world we now live in today. The opportunities for you are now limitless. Long ago, one emotion sprouted an idea, that idea germinated into a thought, and that thought bloomed into a grand decision, and ultimately, an action created results and fulfilled the missing piece in this marvelous puzzle we now call Earth. Take action on your goals, today! Do it now.

1.5 Summary and Execution

1. Write down the most important goals you want to achieve within the following year.
2. Write down what you can do to achieve your goals and do something every day that will propel you closer to completing that goal.
3. Only watch, study, and learn the necessary material that will enrich your mental state of mind and help you move forward on your goals that you have set for yourself.
4. Discipline yourself to be available to accomplish your goals: Create a time planner, a blueprint of your goals.
5. Become a goal-oriented person, make it a daily habit, and reap the benefits.
6. You must be willing to sacrifice your time for what is more important to you, right now, tomorrow, and in the future.
7. Take immediate action, today, tomorrow, and every day of the year if you want massive, positive, and life-changing results.

CHAPTER 2

Have a Mission

An Overview

A person without a mission in life will not know where they will end up in the future. You must create and mentally visualize your mission. Your mission will consist of many goals, many obstacles, and many winning or losing situations in your life; therefore, you must have a mission in place.

Without a mission, you are living a life of chance. Write out a plan, brainstorm ideas, create a map of your life and the things, people, the career, and anything else that you want and need to fulfill this mission. We only have one life to live, so live to the fullest of your capabilities—in this beautiful and abundant world. Leap forward and take action, immediately.

2.1 Technique 1: Your Emotions

Every person in this world does not feel and have the same mission as you do. No two people in this world think alike, act identical, or even want the same things for that matter. Is there an emotion from deep within that nags at you night and day, metaphorically, screaming for you to change your life and create a mission for yourself, for your family, and for your future? Then, you must act quickly while the emotions are high, active, and intense in your mind. Change is inevitable. Most people ignore their emotions and move on with their life.

You must not be one of them. Do not settle for an average life. Someone once said, "No one has ever found the limit of human potential." The human mind has too much potential, too many ideas, and too many years available for you to let your beautiful mind and its human energy wither away like a flower without sun and water. Decide to do something today to change the outcome of your future and plan out your mission. You deserve a good life, we all do.

2.2 Technique 2: Your Thoughts

Only you can make this leap to change your life. Think differently than others. Find resources that will help you fulfill your mission: videos, seminars, audiobooks, attend conferences, read more books on your desired topic, or study the necessary skills that will benefit you and help you fulfill this mission.

The resources and possibilities to succeed and accomplish your mission are endless, limitless, and not impossible to attain. Remain positive. Remember, all skills are learnable and teachable. Subconsciously, engrain pure and enriching thoughts into your mind. Stay away from negativity while completing your daily, weekly, monthly, or even, your yearly missions. You can do it!

2.3 Technique 3: Your Decisions

What exactly do you want in life? Do you want to gain financial freedom? Do you want a better career? Do you want to live in a better community? Do you want to meet new friends and support systems that can help you complete your mission? Whatever you want in life is attainable, but you must drill positive affirmations into your mind daily, if not, weekly, if not, monthly, if not yearly, but positive affirmation will motivate you to succeed in all aspects of your life.

Decide from now on to think about success, not about poverty. Earl Nightingale once said long ago, "You become what you think about." Most things in life, we have no control over, but we can decide what we think about most of the time. The mind is your most powerful asset and from the moment you were born, it began working. Think about how to complete your mission and take action, today!

2.4 Technique 4: Your Actions

Finally, you must act on your mission. Redefine your success and execute your mission(s). You may begin in increments and slowly succeed and that's okay. The important thing is that you begin. Begin completing one small mission and it will lead you to complete another one and another one and another one. In time, these positive actions will become a wonderful habit. You will gain momentum.

By the time you know it, you will be addicted to succeeding and completing your mission(s), no matter how small or large your mission, there is beauty, there is a sense of satisfaction, and a reward upon completion of every one of your missions. There is always someone watching, listening, and seeking mission-driven people. Become the successful person you are meant to be and take action, today!

2.5 Summary and Execution

1. Define your mission in life and make a plan to commit to that mission every day.
2. Create a mission planner in detail, create a list, and identify your mission on paper: Write it down.
3. Hang up your mission statement somewhere where you can see it every day as a daily reminder.
4. Take small steps or large steps every day to slowly fulfill your mission and before you know it, you will be one step closer to completing your mission.
5. If possible, surround yourself with positive people in a positive environment, and with a positive attitude.
6. Always seek advice, opinions, and trends in your field of interest that will help you, guide you, and push you to complete your mission.
7. Always work hard, communicate effectively, and live as if someone is always watching because you never know when your efforts will be noticed by someone that can offer you an opportunity that can change your life forever.

CHAPTER 3

Be Selfish

An Overview

A person who cannot love the person they have become will not be able to reach their full potential in life. We must get in touch with our inner soul, our body, our mind, and our personality. You have to be selfish in a way that will help you gain the self-confidence you need to grow your self-esteem.

There are many steppingstones in life you must place before you—before you can create a solid foundation of success. Because if we cannot bear to look at ourselves in the mirror every morning and say, "I love myself or I love my life," something is wrong. But do not be discouraged, for you can change the outcome of your life, we all can. Take charge of your life, today.

3.1 Technique 1: Your Emotions

Most people in life wander, disengaged with others, instead, their emotionally connected to their digital devices or they have lost touch with reality, and in most cases, themselves. You, on the other hand, must change the way you feel on the inside before you can get what you want on the outside.

You want more out of life. You want more success out of life. You want to change your current situation. Or, you want to become a stronger, more emotionally individual who can relate to others' mishaps and successes and resonate with the people around you. But to do so, you must love yourself first because, without that innate distinction and quality, you will send mixed messages to your peers, to your family, to your co-workers, and more importantly, to yourself. As a result, you will gain negative energy instead of positive energy.

To reach complete fulfillment and potential in life, we must grasp the love that exists within us and express it to everyone around us—always. Despite whatever others may think of you, feel the love from within yourself and express it to others in a candid way—every day.

3.2 Technique 2: Your Thoughts

The ability to control your thoughts will ultimately define your successes in life. What is it that is stopping you from succeeding? Who is stopping you from thinking positively, genuinely, and authentically? Is your environment slowing you down? Then change it. Stop hanging around in the kind of atmosphere that does not create positive results toward your future success. Why? Because that setting will only create negative thoughts in your mind, negative feelings, negative decisions, and in the end, negative results.

Unfortunately, your mind goes everywhere you do, so take charge of your situation, take charge of your mind, and plan accordingly.

Think before you decide. Think before you make another decision and say to yourself, "Will this environment help me reach my full potential, help me succeed toward my goals, one step closer toward my dreams, aspirations, and achieve success?" Every thought has a consequence. Every action has power behind it. You are powerful, in a sense, because only you can control your thoughts.

Remember, love yourself and others will feel what you feel. Send a good vibe in your surroundings and others will feel it, see it, and embrace it. This emotional intelligence is a leadership quality that all successful leaders use to communicate, connect, and achieve success, but more importantly, they attract positive attention and positive energy from their followers.

3.3 Technique 3: Your Decisions

Decide to change your inner self-thoughts, today. If you open up the love that exists within yourself to others, it will reflect your future success and open doors that you cannot even begin to imagine were even possible to open. Your decision to make a change in this area will impact your work, your family, and ultimately, your future success.

Many people in this world cannot love themselves for various reasons: they are too poor and live in poverty, permanently; they are orphans and cannot live with that fact, a family member has died, and they cannot cope with that death for the rest of their lives, and the list goes on and on. But hear this, you can rise from adversity, love yourself even more, and conquer your goals.

If other people have risen from nothing to become wealthy and self-made millionaires, so can you. To be successful is not impossible, it consists of hard work and discipline, but I repeat—not impossible. Take action, today, and love yourself for doing so, and watch the positive impact that follows your actions day-by-day. You will be astonished at the results. You can do this!

3.4 Technique 4: Your Actions

Finally, to begin this journey of loving yourself more than you can possibly imagine, you must gain empathy toward others. Feel their pain, feel their loss, feel their emptiness inside their heart and try to fill that hole for them, connect with them if you can. You must resonate with others and understand that you are not alone in this world.

Many have suffered, many have cried, many have died, many have been lonely, or whatever the case may be, many people in this world are afraid to express their love to others for the mere reason that they might be rejected or looked down upon: Do not be that kind of person.

If someone needs you to listen to them, take the time to hear them. If someone needs your help and they are elderly, help them. Don't turn your cheek at them, hold their hand. You gain a touch of humanism more than you can imagine was possible. Help others in a time of need. Sometimes simplicity, time, and a little respect for others can help you love yourself even more.

Psychologically, this cannot be explained but it is true. The mere act of showing compassion for others will increase your love, not only for them but for yourself. Your actions will define you. Do something today, and in time, you shall reap the reward.

3.5 Summary and Execution

1. Become in touch with your inner self: Write down your thoughts, ideas, anything your heart desires. Journaling sometimes conjures up solutions to our situations in life.
2. Take a time out from this busy world and self-reflect on your failures, your struggles, and your accomplishments; only then, will you realize what is working and what is hindering you from achieving more success. Meditation can sometimes help: 30 to 60 minutes a day for yourself.
3. Place yourself in the correct environment, an environment that will allow you to grow: personally, professionally, and spiritually.
4. When you realize that other people in this world are going through or have gone through the same thing you are, this fact alone can help you gain a stronger empathy, compassion, and an appreciation while you pursue your own success.
5. You will gain a sense of satisfaction and self-fulfillment when you speak, talk, and think more positively on a daily basis.
6. Always respect the elderly, volunteer where possible, help out someone when possible, or do something that can change the lives of others and reap the benefits of becoming a leader by helping those less fortunate than you.
7. All in all, become self-conscious of your actions, yourself, and your environment: If you do not like something in your life, change it.

CHAPTER 4

Be Responsible

An Overview

A n individual who lives their life without thinking about
the consequences of their actions, has no direct or definite
plan, has no goals, or objectives lined up for their future, is
destined for failure. You must take charge of your actions.

Remember, whatever you do now, will impact the rest of your
life. You must think hard, think smart. And every time you need to
make a huge decision in your life, think of the short-term as well as
the long-term consequences. Most people in life think of the short-
term gain and instead, experience long-term pain because of their

inability to react maturely, responsibly, and concisely. We must take full responsibility for our actions.

You must clear your mind from negative thoughts and veer them toward positive actions. You must value your life now, for yesterday is history. A professor once said, "Do something now that will make a difference in your life because yesterday is history: Yesterday is gone. More importantly, you can never get that time or day back." So take responsibility for your actions today, for tomorrow is another marvelous and spectacular day—if—you want it to be.

4.1 Technique 1: Your Emotions

Most people in life make horrible decisions at the beginning of their lives. However, most individuals are not at fault for making such bad decisions. The cause of their actions was their upbringing, maybe it was their race, their environment, and/or their current situation. Unfortunately, the list can go on and on.

As a result, we blame ourselves and this is a measly way to live. You must not live with this mindset. Psychologically, blaming yourself will hurt you physically, emotionally, and mentally and it will diminish your chances of being all you can be, being successful and reaching your full potential.

Do not individualize yourself from others as irresponsible; instead, embrace and change your life, now! Do not have a negative mindset and believe you cannot succeed, for you will fail before you even start your journey toward a successful future. Try to feel as if you are the most responsible person you have ever met in this world and trick yourself into believing that on a daily basis: Reprogram your mind.

Choose to embark on a new path toward the enrichment of your life. Change your actions, today. Make the leap toward a better, smarter, and decisive you. Take responsibility for your actions—one day at a time, one decision at a time, and one powerful thought at a time. You can do this!

4.2 Technique 2: Your Thoughts

There is nothing more important than having done something and being penalized for your actions. Someone once asked a question: What is the hardest thing there is to do in life? "To Think," they said. Many people do not take the time to examine their thoughts and the consequences can be disastrous and life-changing. You must think hard, think smart, and think like a successful individual even if you do not yet have the wealth or the financial freedom you desire. Think of your consequences before taking action on anything you do, buy, or watch, see or hear.

But when you do decide on something you want, take action fast so you can gain momentum swiftly. Remember, think fast, fail faster, and you will succeed quicker. But the point here is, you need to gain momentum.

Single-mindedly, at all times, have your major goal in your mind and let those thoughts marinate in your conscious, and subconsciously, your choices will become better every day.

I cannot explain this phenomenon, but your ability to engrain positive thoughts in your mind will be the determiner of your successes in life. Success does not happen by accident but by executing smart and decisive actions and reaping the consequences of your efforts. Take action, today. Transform your goals and experience the difference, today. We must be responsible and take charge of our thoughts: Change your thoughts and you will change your outcomes in life.

4.3 Technique 3: Your Decisions

From this day on, decide to take full responsibility for your actions. If you can control your emotions before making a decision, the more positive and concise your decision will turn out. If you can be responsible, mature, and strong-minded, and you do not let the mere, negative pure pressures in life control your mind, your actions will define your ultimate success. Use the power of emotional intelligence, the ability to examine your emotions, the emotions of others, and why you are feeling the way you are feeling.

Next time you have a decision to make, choose to think clearly and see into the future, first. Visualize, if you are willing, the consequences of your actions. All successful and high-performance men and women think before they act. Business leaders think about the future of their company; they think about their products, they think about their employees, they think about their finances, but more importantly, they think about their customers. The list of details can go on and on about the importance of decision-making, but the point here is, the decisions you make now can either nourish your success or hinder it. You have the power. You are responsible. You are the greatest person in your life, so take full responsibility and take advantage of your once-in-a-lifetime opportunities that come your way: positively, responsibly, and with integrity.

Initially, all the greatest inventions in and above this world began with someone deciding to act upon their ideas, their goals, examined their hypotheses, and ultimately, they failed many times before they became successful. The point here is, few will truly succeed in life and accomplish their goals because they wasted their time choosing and using alcohol, experimenting with drugs, and they never thought about the consequences. Those few who do succeed in life, are clear about what they want, why they want it, and how to get it—every day.

We must be responsible. We must think about the outcomes of our actions, will they benefit us or hurt us. Before you do anything in life, think about the consequences before you take action in all aspects of your life. You can do this.

4.4 Technique 4: Your Actions

Finally, if there is anything in life you should keenly remain aware of at all times, it is your actions: are they helping you are slowing you down? Are you gaining followers or are you creating enemies, metaphorically speaking? Just as the sun rises and sets, your actions begin and end in a positive or negative consequence.

You may not always succeed in accomplishing your goals in the beginning, but mark my words, if you wake up every day with pizazz and positive energy, you will achieve the success you are so hungry for every day. Some days may be harder than other days, but as long as you are creating positive actions, you are creating momentum.

As long as you take full responsibility for what you have done and do not blame others, you will succeed in all aspects of your life. We must not blame the government, or blame our negative relatives, or anyone else for that matter. Success begins on the inside of you, not on the outside. Become a responsible individual, become a leader of your life, become the best person you can be, for everyone has greatness within them.

Take charge of your life and the greatness that exists within you. Control it, examine it, and nourish it. Become self-aware of your responsibilities in life and separate yourself from the average individual that just lives a life of mediocrity.

But remember, if you unconsciously make many small bad decisions, you will experience long-term failures. Create new beneficial habits, powerful actions, and others will feed off your positive energy too. Remember, actions really do speak louder than words, let yours be heard and felt across the world without any regrets. You can do this!

4.5 Summary and Execution

1. The day you take full responsibility for your actions, will be the day you will realize and create more potential success and accelerate your full potential capabilities.
2. If you take small actions, you will receive small rewards. But if you take massive actions, you will reap huge rewards.
3. Always think about your consequences before performing an action: this concept will save you time, fewer heartaches, expand your personal and professional relationships, and of course, create more wealth in your life.
4. If you will examine your failures as well as your successes in your life, you will make better decisions for the future, execute stronger actions, and you will initially become more responsible.
5. Take responsibility for your actions, understand the potential consequences that follow them, and reap the rewards of your hard efforts—or suffer the penalty for being irresponsible.
6. Remember, most people will accept short-term gain, but they will receive long-term pain: Do not fall into this category.
7. Take control of your life, if not others will control it for you.

CHAPTER 5

Take a Risk

An Overview

A major difference that distinguishes successful individuals from the average everyday person, is the fact that a successful person continuously looks for the next opportunity, regardless of the failure that may come with that opportunity. Meanwhile, the average person is fear-stricken and will never decide to make that next step and take a chance at his or her success. You have so much potential. You have so many brain cells within your mind; therefore, the power is within the mind; you have more power than you can possibly imagine. "So use it or lose it."

For you to become highly successful, change your current situation, or even, begin to change your life, you must face your fears and take a risk. Take a chance, overcome difficulties in order to see massive possibilities in your life. Open doors that you have never tried to open before and walk through them and be amazed by what is on the other side.

You never know who you are going to meet. You never know when and where your next big idea is going to become a reality if you do not risk anything. Think about how much you actually risk every day for the sake of doing what you love, your passion, the one big thing that brings you satisfaction on a daily basis.

Think hard about it. What would you love to do if you knew you had all the time in the world, all the resources and the financial freedom to do it every day for the rest of your life? What is your passion? This thought alone will help you think about your next steps toward living a more prosperous and meaningful life.

5.1 Technique 1: Your Emotions

Millions of people every day take a risk without even thinking—and others for the wrong reasons. If you can think about your success and visualize yourself already being successful, this alone will help you, encourage you, and push you toward taking a greater risk. See yourself as a risk-taker. You have a higher probability of accomplishing the goals you set for yourself if you challenge yourself, set bigger goals, and set higher expectations for yourself.

In the process, you will increase your confidence, your self-esteem, and as a result, you will try more things. We all want more out of life, so think big. Think big and your reward will be huge. If you are taking a small risk, your reward will be insignificant.

All successful people, entrepreneurs, and high-achievers take a risk, they capitalize and dominate their obstacles. They fail and succeed. The secret is, to realize that we all fail, we all have problems, but it is how we deal with those problems that determines our future and our success.

You may fail but get back up. Talk to a different person, visit a different company, experience a different environment, and the list of new possibilities can go on and on. Create your future and watch opportunities unfold before you. If you never failed at anything in life, you never did anything in life.

If your emotions are telling you to attempt something new in your life, go with that gut feeling. Challenge yourself and take that risk, today. Decide to change your ventures, today. Take action, today, and do not be amazed by the opportunities that will arise in your life, today. You can do it, today!

5.2 Technique 2: Your Thoughts

Many people live their lives without taking a risk because they set their standards so low that they fail to reach their full potential. As a result, they are not excited, aroused, or motivated to pursue their dreams and aspirations. You must not be that kind of person.

Set "Standards of Excellence," think about your future, and isolate yourself from negative attention, negative goals, and people that are not willing to risk anything. Most people are content with the life they have been given, but you must rise and never settle for average in order to fulfill your passion, your dreams, and all of your major goals in life. Never give up! Never give in and never settle for average when you can become greater in your field of interest.

If you can think and truly believe that you can succeed toward your next project, your subconscious, your inner brain, and your body will guide you. Do not be afraid before you even start, for there is nothing to be afraid of. We live in a country of opportunity. And when you can get yourself to think of opportunity, success, and your future— simultaneously, you will realize that along, all you needed to do was take a risk.

Focus your thoughts on what you want out of life instead of what you do not have. Honestly, you cannot grow if you cannot change. Take a chance and jump at the next opportunity that flies by your way. Control your thoughts: Do it now and reap the rewards in abundances.

5.3 Technique 3: Your Decisions

Many decide to never change their lives and instead, live an average life. Don't settle for plain and simple. You, your family, your grandkids, and your future deserve better. If you decide on anything, today, decide to change your current path toward growing and becoming more successful.

If you have changed your current situation and want more opportunities, then seek out a mentor who you admire and shadow them. Decide to learn everything you possibly can in your field of interest because any skill is learnable. Ask more questions, send a positive post, create a positive message on your blog, upgrade your website, change your social media content, or make a phone call and speak to someone that may change your life in an instant. Study another language, or whatever your heart desires, just decide to do it, today. Do not wait, for yesterday is history. Decide to change, today and make yourself more valuable to the marketplace.

Squeeze in the time into your busy schedule and take a risk that otherwise you would have never attempted. Precision decision-making is a key factor in the business world. All high-performance individuals, high-achievers, leaders, and all goal-oriented people take a risk. You can too. Become meticulous when taking risks and take a chance toward a more successful life, today.

5.4 Technique 4: Your Actions

Finally, do not be discouraged by the people who have told you that you will never amount to anything. Instead, use that negativity as motivation and push through that obstacle and quickly move on with your life. Stay away from them.

You must take action to remain around people that want you to succeed. You must act, now. You must take risks where others are afraid to because of a lack of self-confidence and self-esteem. At the end of the day, your actions will define you and your future success.

You may not know when other people are watching, but believe me, someone is always watching. Get the attention of your superiors, get the attention of those in your desired field. Get the attention of those who you so much want to compete with. You have to sell yourself every day. That is the name of the game.

You are an asset; the more you know, the higher you progress in life, and the more people you will meet. As a result, you will gain more opportunities. Create your own brand, throw yourself out there to the world and see what happens. We learn and get what we want by taking action and seeing what happens. But, if you do not act on your gut-feeling, no one will do it for you.

You are wonderful; you are smart, and if you are reading this, you are already on the right path toward enriching your life with positive and mental protein because you want more, you deserve more, and you will do everything in your power to succeed and learn more. Never give up!

Continue your journey toward a more successful and abundant life of taking chances and reap the rewards of your courage and persistence. Remember, if you never failed at anything in life, you never did anything in life. Change that, today. Take action, today!

5.5 Summary and Execution

1. Be a smart risk-taker and follow your gut-feeling when an idea arises; write that idea down in your journal, pursue it (the goal), think of strategies (make a plan), and implement your goal to become a reality (take action to achieve that goal).
2. Quickly pursue your idea. Do not let your idea slip away from your mind. Capture it. Write it down. Do not let your mind be a file cabinet.
3. Visit other environments, talk to other people in your desired field of interest and take a chance. You never know who you might meet.
4. Do not let other people discourage you, stay away from negativity, non-growing environments, and situations that will not help you and your ideas, dreams, and goals reach their full potential.
5. It is important to allocate the necessary time to experiment with the new endeavors you so much want to try out.
6. Remember, if you fail, try and try again because the most successful people and the biggest companies in the world never succeeded on the first try. It was their continuous persistence to never give up on their dreams that amounted to massive success.
7. Where there is an opportunity, there will be difficulties. When you realize this concept alone, you will accept and overcome difficulties and learn from them instead of quitting. Do not give up, do not hinder, and take a risk, because if you never failed at anything in your life, you never did anything in your life: Learn, live, and conquer and create success in your life, today.

CHAPTER 6

Face Adversity

> *Letting life knock you down without getting back up is a recipe for failure.*
>
> -Les Brown

An Overview

A person who cannot overcome adversity is destined to remain unpowerful and unable to face any of life's challenges. You must accept the fact that life is power-charged by failures before success can dominate the next course of action. The only difference is; will you be around to experience those misfortunes? Will you learn from your failures? Will you be able to push through the adversities that occur in your life?

If so, you are the fortunate one. Gain more experience, become detailed-oriented, and fail and succeed. Over time, you will learn what not to do, when to do it, and how to overcome hardships in the future.

Knowing how to face adversity, overcome it, and deal with it from an emotional standpoint, will determine your overall personal success. Don't let life's challenges knock you down, upset you, or corral your emotions with negativity, for these actions will kill any chances for you to succeed in all aspects of your life.

Instead, learn from your difficulties, examine them, create a plan, and take action immediately. We must learn from our mistakes and use those experiences as wisdom to succeed in all aspects of our lives. Unfortunately, many people never discover or explore more success in their lives. Why?

Why do some people challenge themselves and others do not? This is a universal question which I do not have the answer to. Simply, some do, and some do not. You must not fall into this category. Never give up and believe that there is always a solution to any problem in your life.

6.1 Technique 1: Your Emotions

Sadly, it is a fact that millions of people suffer more because they have experienced some sort of hardship. Their emotional state overpowers their state of mind for years to come, and ultimately, they choose to never resolve their current situation, they never try to become more resourceful, and they never overcome their adversities. As a result, they fall into the system—a never-ending cycle of poverty.

Problems will arise in your life, but it is knowing how to solve these problems and move on with your life that will ultimately define you as a person, strengthen your character, and help you succeed in all aspects of life.

We all have problems, but it is how we deal with them that classifies us as leaders in our field of interest. In the end, your reaction to those problems will demonstrate your true character, gain more positive attention, and opportunities.

Do not remain in a state of shock for the rest of your life, for you will miss the chance at being successful and achieving any other goals you have set for yourself. So discipline yourself to not let your feelings overpower you, render you, and control you.

Examples of adversities: the death of a family member, mourn and use that; you failed to get the job you wanted, know why, and go learn more skills in that field; you have not bought the house of your dreams, visualize that property and create a solid foundation and generate a plan on how to get that house. This list can go on and on. Remember though, difficulties can create motivation and inspiration.

The solutions toward your successes are not impossible, they are learnable. But if you cannot face adversity and continue positively with your life, your difficulties will impact your emotions, your emotions will impact your thoughts, your thoughts will impact your decisions, and ultimately, your decisions will impact the most important aspect of you—your actions!

Change your emotional state when you confront adversities, rise and succeed to the next level, and experience the positive impact it can have on your life, today, tomorrow, and for the rest of your life.

6.2 Technique 2: Your Thoughts

Millions of people across the world face adversities and think they cannot ever overcome or change their current situation. Truly, many never do change their situation, and for that reason, they never reach their full potential in life.

If you think you cannot succeed, you will not. If think you cannot ever challenge yourself more than once, you will not. If you think you cannot bounce back from problems, you are wrong. If you think that you are the only one in this world facing problems, you are wrong. Think abroad and think global.

We all have difficulties, but the true key to overcoming these adversities, is to push forward and do not listen to the naysayers. You can change your current situation by simply controlling your thoughts. After a strong defeat in life, surround yourself only with positive energy, not negative energy, and notice the difference. This alone can change your life.

Decide and conquer your true potential one step at a time. Believe in yourself and accept adversities as a learning experience and a chance for new opportunities, not a brick wall that will stop you from pursuing your dreams, your goals, and your aspirations. Jim

Rohn once said, "Life is the mixture of opportunities and difficulties; life is like the changing seasons, opportunity follows difficulty." Your job is to decide to take advantage when the spring, summer, fall, and winter comes along.

Winston Churchill once said long ago, "The pessimist sees difficulty in every opportunity, but the optimist sees opportunity in every difficulty." Make the right choice, today! Become a critical thinker and expand your full potential and decide to accept problems as they come, and they will. So, as the late Jim Rohn once said: "Do not ask for less problems, ask for more skills," more knowledge, and more wisdom to help you reach your full potential in all aspects of your life.

6.3 Technique 3: Your Decisions

Decide to fight back when problems arise. Decide to fight back with your mind. Learn and reflect on the mishaps that you will encounter throughout your personal, professional, and / or academic journey toward a more successful life.

Do not overlook the opportunities that await you when one door is slammed in your face, that only means another one will open. If someone tells you—you cannot achieve success, then, make the important decision to talk to someone that thinks otherwise. No two people in this world think alike, so find a second or third or fourth or even, a fifth opinion. Eventually, the first steppingstone and your chance at a life-changing opportunity will arise. You just have to decide to stay positive and never give up on your dreams, your goals in life, and more importantly, never give up on yourself.

If you have problems, decide to not stop seeking solutions to those problems. Never give up! Never quit. Never take your first failure as exactly what it is, failure. Instead, embrace that disappointment, revisit your past actions and do not repeat them.

Simply restructure your life according to your plans for the future: push past adversity, welcome difficulties, and challenge yourself more and more every day. Your future depends on the decisions that you make every day, so take the time to think and reflect, and if you do, your life will change. You can do this!

6.4 Technique 4: Your Actions

Finally, it is your mindset and the actions that you will take after a problem occurs in your personal or professional life that defines you. Embrace the reality that situations will happen in the workplace, but knowing how to face them, will separate you from the average person.

If you get knocked down, get back up even stronger. If you get knocked down—again, get back up even smarter. And if you get knocked down again, get back up even faster. Take the necessary action and learn all you need to know.

Study the books, watch the seminars, watch or listen to the videos, and any other instructional material that can help you develop physically and spiritually. If you cannot understand something in school, at home, or in a business atmosphere, take the time to study, reflect, and research that theory. Change your philosophy and change your life, today.

If you feel that you cannot succeed in life for whatever reason, seek advice, help, and, if possible, seek a mentor who will advise you, guide you, and help you reach your full potential quicker. Mostly all successful people have mentors and coaches so do not be intimidated.

When you realize that others have encountered the same challenges you have, you will be more optimistic about accomplishing your ultimate goal, and in fact, you will come across more resources, too. The possibilities and resources in this time and age—are limitless. Take action on your goals, and take action, now, for yesterday is history.

6.5 Summary and Execution

1. Opportunity follows difficulty and vice-versa. You will experience them during the seasons: Spring, summer, fall, and winter, so be ready.

2. Everyone has problems in life: Business leaders, politicians, the rich and the poor and the list goes on and on. But it is how you deal with your problems that defines you and shows your true character.

3. If you can control your emotional state when a problem arises, you will learn the art of emotional intelligence. The ability to become more self-aware of your actions, your feelings, and the emotions of those around you. This is a leadership quality.

4. Millions of people fall into a state of mind of defeat and never pursue their aspirations in life. Never give up on your dreams and accept defeats: examine them, learn from them, and take action immediately.

5. Never give up, never listen to naysayers, negativity, and unconstructive behavior. Follow your gut-feeling and strive for success, fortune, and financial freedom. Face adversity with courage and be ready.

6. If you get knocked down, get back up even stronger, get back up even smarter, get back up even faster, and take massive action immediately.

7. Failure is temporary, but your success will last a lifetime. Always fight back, seek out mentors, focus and create a strong mindset that will help you overcome problems when they arise. Say to yourself whenever necessary: "Failure is not an option." Remember, repetition is the mother of skill.

CHAPTER 7

Courage

> *You will never do anything in this world without courage. It is the greatest quality of the mind next to honor. Courage is the first of human qualities because it is the quality which guarantees the others.*
>
> -Aristotle

An Overview

Courage cannot be defined by the wit of others, but by your willingness to overcome the fear from within and stride forward in all aspects of your life. You must conquer all obstacles and challenges that get in your way. Challenges may obstruct you, but courage will dominate them.

Your ability to fight for what you want in life is the essential force that pushes you toward your future success. Maybe there is a job position at work, for example, that others do not dare to apply for because they are frightened by the responsibilities that accompany that position and title. You should always experience something for yourself before believing someone else. The worst thing that can happen is that you may fail; nonetheless, with failure comes knowledge and experience and opportunity.

Also, when you win, accept it, but when you lose, learn from it before you push it away. Be brave, strong, and willing to get up to fight another day. Be courageous by all means necessary. Someone once said, "Pain does not last forever." Use the pain in any situation to your advantage; thereafter, seek out other opportunities quickly.

You must think highly of yourself and always be willing to take the next leap forward and experiment and create new opportunities for yourself. In many cases, no one will take you by the hand and lead you to your success. So you have to be courageous, ruthless, but smart about it; you must want more goodness, better health and more wealth out of life and have the courage to defeat your inner demons.

If you settle for average work, you will receive average pay. If you settle for an average life, you will be seen as an average individual. As a result, you will not attract success. Be bold, be strong, be brave; be all that you can possibly be with this one life that you have been given. Remember, "Every day is a gift."

We only live once so make the best of it. Be responsible, take control of your life, think about your success, and settle for nothing less.

Remember, big projects can become big opportunities for advancement in any position or job title. While small and minute projects attract minor opportunities for advancement. Think big and you will be rewarded big. Think small and you will be rewarded small.

In the end, we need to think smart, think about possibilities and opportunities, think about our success, be brave and confident, in the sense, that you can achieve anything you put your mind to. You are powerful and your mind is your greatest asset, so use it or you lose it.

7.1 Technique 1: Your Emotions

Millions of people are brave but do not always make the right decisions. Most people follow their intuition for the wrong reasons. You must know what you want in life and do everything in your power to get it. Do not let the emotions of others interfere with your emotions, your goals, your plans, and your actions to live a better and more successful life. There is greatness within you, unleash it.

There are two types of brave people in this world; those that are brave but not smart and those that are super smart and not courageous enough to take action on their goals.

For example, a petty bank robber who has the courage to rob the bank; he feels no remorse. He steals the money, and he escapes.

In comparison, another brave person feels deep down in their heart that they have the greatest idea that can help them generate success; they are talented, they have the necessary skills, but they lack the one quality that can change their lives . . . "Courage!"

So move forward, overcome your fears, and pursue your dreams. Many people in this world will hinder you from accomplishing your own goals if you let them. Be brave and learn to say no. Do not let your emotions get the best of you. Stay away from negativity.

If anything, the negative emotions of others will only delay your future success because of the lack of courage they have to overcome their adversities. Have you ever been around someone negative? Have you ever been around someone who dislikes success? They will delay your own success if you let them. They are called "Dream stealers."

As a result, they will only bring you down with them. They will ultimately live in a plague of weakness for the rest of their lives. Do not be a follower, be a leader and student of your own success. Take charge of your emotions, take charge of your life, and take charge of your own goals, today! You can do this.

You must remain outgoing and stand out from the others in your workplace in order to rise in the ranks and be paid more if that is what you desire. Be courageous and reap the reward of your positive and brave actions, but more importantly, become self-aware, those inner thoughts, that gut feeling that guides you: Feel it and listen to it. We sometimes call it "Intuition."

Nevertheless, keep moving forward in life, moving toward your personal and financial goals. Be instinctive and strengthen your courage in the process. In time, you will realize that being courageous is an essential steppingstone in becoming a higher performer and a more influential asset to your organization, to your business, and ultimately—in all aspects of your own life. Be courageous and do something that will forever change your life and experience your life in a totally different way. Live your life to the fullest; live your life with a purpose. Inevitably, you will develop physically, mentally, and emotionally.

7.2 Technique 2: Your Thoughts

Many people live their lives thinking they have reached their limit in life. But no one has ever found the limit of human potential. Do not be fooled by what you see and hear. Do not be misguided. Always search for the facts.

We all want to live longer, think smarter, create more opportunities, create more success, and gain more courage to do what is necessary to succeed in all aspects of life. Do not let fear hold you back. Do not let the fear of being rejected intimidate you, either.

Fear kills dreams. Fear kills hope. Fear can age you. Fear puts people in the hospitals. Fear is the most destructive of all human diseases and Les Brown adds: Fear can hold you from doing something that you are capable of doing and it will paralyze you if you let, knock you on your knees and keep you there if you let it. Overcome your fear for "You have nothing to fear but fear itself."

Your mindset can hinder you before you even begin to think about accumulating wealth. Having the courage to take action is the #1 reason why millions of people do not reach their full potential in life or acquire abundances of wealth.

If you are led to believe that you can only live a life of poverty under the circumstances of living check-to-check or hypnotized by the power of welfare, then that will be your overall thoughts and your mindset. Change the way you think, and you will change the way you live. Accept only positive thoughts to linger in your mind.

When negative thoughts arise, quickly replace them with positive affirmations that you say to yourself on a daily basis until you have reprogrammed your mind to think about wealth and happiness. This may seem foolish, but it works.

It has been said, "You become what you think about most of the time." Think about success and you will want it.

We will never progress in life or conquer adversities in the workplace without courage. Raise yourself from obscurity and a low-level mindset of thinking and watch as opportunities begin to cross your path.

Do something out of the ordinary, today, and your self-confidence will grow. Your mind will grow, your ideas will grow, and your overall potential will grow, too.

7.3 Technique 3: Your Decisions

If you can do anything, decide to be more courageous. Take the time to think about how you can show others that you are not weak. Take a chance in life. Climb that mountain you have wanted to for so long; drive in your vehicle and take a road-trip; fly in a plane to another country with someone or by yourself; apply for that job you have been thinking about for so long, and do it, now! Just do something and gain momentum: create more energy.

Don't think about the results at the current moment or the "What if" things do not turn out as I wanted. Then, move on. If you want to buy something, buy it. If you like something, get it without thinking twice about it. If you want to talk to that potential prospect, do it.

You never know what can happen if you just throw yourself out there into the world of business and see what happens. The results may surprise you.

Eventually, the more things you try, the more momentum you gain in life, and more importantly, the better your chances are at succeeding rather than having done nothing at all. Try nothing and you will receive nothing.

Either way, your decisions will amount to momentum, and when you gain momentum, you gain knowledge and new experiences, and when you gain new experiences, you gain more self-confidence, and when you gain more confidence, your self-esteem rises. As a result, you gain more courage without even knowing it.

In time, being courageous will become natural and automatic. Your confidence will grow; your income will grow, and your personal development will grow.

The benefits of bravery and smart decision-making are so satisfying that others will think you are crazy. Do not be discouraged by what other people might think of you. Be bold, be brave, and make an insatiable and courageous impact in your life, today. You can do it!

7.4 Technique 4: Your Actions

Finally, in the end, the actions that you will take in your life will ultimately define you. There are no courageous losers, only courageous winners. No one ever won the Olympics by staying home and drowning themselves in self-pity. No one ever won an NBA championship by acting weak. No country ever won a war without courageous individuals who sacrificed their lives for the freedoms that we now enjoy.

All high-performers and CEOs take action whether they fail or not, they continue and do not stop until they have won, until they have gotten to the top. And when they have gotten to the top, they quickly think about how to remain there, how to remain successful. For them, the rest is automatic as they repeat the process over and over.

Someone once said, "Repetition is the mother of all success and repetition is the mother of all skills." What must you repeat to become more successful? Will you study more? Will you speak to a mentor more often? Will you blog more, write more, or communicate more effectively? What? Discover what it is that you must continue to do on a daily basis in order to become highly successful and you will be. Decide to change, today. Find your strengths, minimize your weaknesses, take action, study, learn all you need to know, and repeat the process over and over until you reach ultimate success in your life.

Taking action is the key to all successes in life. Positive results are what you want in your life to develop into a high-performance-driven individual. But remember, we need to feed off of other highly successful individuals, learn from them, learn out to think like them, learn to see what they see, learn to hear what they hear, read what they read, and then have the courage to take all that we have learned and use it to help us become more successful.

Actions really do speak louder than words. Remember, success leaves clues, so follow the bread trail, the paper trail, and "Follow the Money." Be brave and call that mentor, set up that interview, or whatever it takes in order to raise your success to the next level. Take action on your dreams and aspirations, today! You can do this one piece at a time, one step at a time, and one good idea at a time.

7.5 Summary and Execution

1. The courage to try new things in the workplace, at home, in your state, in your community, or trying new ideas will build up your self-esteem.

2. Some people always say, you only live once, but they never try anything new. Stay away from those people; instead, find someone who can help you, guide you, and encourage you.

3. Follow your intuition, whenever you see something you want, buy it. You want to talk to that potential prospect, do it. The results may surprise you.

4. Never take no for an answer, if someone says no, go somewhere else. Eventually, someone will say yes. This world is too big and with the capabilities and technology available for you—you are bound to find someone that loves your idea, your services, your invention, or your product. Never give up!

5. The time to begin will never be perfect, so start as soon as possible. Be brave, courageous, strong, and remain disciplined to do what is necessary.

6. In the end, your actions will define you. You will build a reputation for being the person that gets things done, not scared to try new things, talk to new prospects, and go the extra mile.

7. Finally, your ability to learn from other high-driven individuals will help you: Learn from them. Remember, success leaves clues. Ask questions and become a good listener. Eventually, courage will become natural to you, and you will attract success, for "Success is something you attract, not achieve" (Jim Rohn). So become more attractive and valuable to the marketplace by learning new things.

CHAPTER 8

Standards of Excellence

—❝———

One reason so few of us achieve what we truly want is that we never direct our focus; we never concentrate our power. Most people dabble their way through life, never deciding to master anything in particular.

-Tony Robbins

———❞—

An Overview

Most people do not set high standards of excellence for themselves. For whatever reason, many individuals underestimate the power of their own mind; as a result, they will never reach their full potential in life.

Plan to make your dreams a reality. Brainstorm and associate your future success with the success of others. Master what is possible, for nothing is impossible. You need not fly across the world to have someone tell you that you are special, smart, and full of talent. Just know this, everything that you need to succeed in life is above your shoulders—the beautiful and the fully unexamined mind. Your mind!

Create and dominate the high expectations that you set for yourself and watch as your brain takes over and commands excellence: Your job is to execute those commands without fear. Set high standards of excellence for yourself and watch as your potential develops. You can do this!

8.1 Technique 1: Your Emotions

Most people in life are emotionally satisfied. Some live life passively, some live lazily, some live comfortably, and others just do not care how they live. Some work every day, while others dream big. Who knows why some people never take action or set great expectations for themselves, but this is part of life? Please, do not be placed in this category.

We must set the bar high, think high, not low, think big, fail big, succeed big. Continue to live high and sore with the eagles, metaphorically speaking. Persist! Persist! and persist until you are satisfied. Reach above and beyond your limits. Set high expectations for yourself and raise your confidence, your astuteness, and your self-awareness.

Gain the emotional strength to fulfill your dreams, your aspirations, and your overall goals. Gain an emotional balance that will drive you, move you, and an emotional balance that will satisfy and encourage you to commit and complete all that you want out of life.

If you are willing to set high expectations for yourself, you will reap the rewards and accomplish more success. Follow your emotions and embrace the thoughts that come to your mind. Visualize yourself already successful. Feel confident and think high and anchor yourself down, and take the time to focus and understand why you want more success, that is, if you haven't gotten a taste of success already.

A huge technique that can help you become more selfaware of your emotional intelligence and your desires, is the ability to meditate for as long as needed. Listen to positive meditation sounds, connect with your mind alone, connect with your body alone, connect with your inner thoughts in serenity, and meditate in a quiet place so that you can reflect on your goals. The reward will be astonishing. Do this every day for one hour for one month and experience the difference in your emotional attitude toward others as well as yourself. Refine your daily schedule as needed.

Take the time to absorb your successes and your failures, but do not linger on the failures too long. Keep pushing forward and when you feel like giving up, push yourself even harder.

Become emotionally but not physically connected with the great things in life: family, work, play, and money. Do not let your emotions stop you from reaching your full potential in life. If you can control your emotions, you will control your future. If not, someone will control your emotions for you: Mass media and its advertisements, for example, and the list can go on and on.

Find your emotional strengths and dominate them, use them. Use your emotional strengths to the best of your ability and overcome adversities.

And if you carefully control your emotions, your thoughts will impact your decisions, and your actions will guide you automatically towards a more bountiful life for you and your family. Change and raise your expectations in life and change them, now! and reap the benefits of your hard work, your dedication, your self-discipline, and do not be surprised when new opportunities come your way; instead, embrace them. You can do this!

8.2 Technique 2: Your Thoughts

Many people live a life of low-level thinking. They never stretch their imagination or demonstrate their higher power. In truth, we never fully use the capabilities that are created by the mind. Supposedly, according to research and surveys, people only use 10 to 20 percent of their potential. The rest of our potential is constantly flowing through billions of neurons, through billions of cells in the brain, intertwining with thousands of thoughts.

Your mind and your thoughts together are marvelous, capable of assisting you to succeed in all aspects of your life. Gain control of your thoughts and you will gain control of your life.

Every person on Earth has the number one tool to succeed in this world, and that tool is—their mind. Learn to condition your mind, your thoughts, and embrace the reality that you have the power to change anything in your life that you want. The change will take time of course, but your time and the days on this Earth are going to pass by anyway, so take advantage, today.

Many people exercise and condition their bodies but not their minds. Think about setting high standards of excellence for yourself and take the next step to exercise your mind. Reprogram your mind and if you are willing, do this on a daily basis. You can do this!

There are many techniques available on how to eliminate negative thoughts and how to replace them with positive thoughts. Choose the techniques that best suits you, for no two people are alike in this world. Make the change, today. Decide what you want and how to get it. All successful people always have one main goal in their minds at all times. They think about what they want and how to get it.

You too must think this way. Know what you want and how to get it!

This is so important that I want to repeat this: You must know what you want and work on it every day, just a little bit, every week, every month of the year until you get what you want. Never give up!

8.3 Technique 3: Your Decisions

If you can decide on anything, raise your standards, raise your expectations, measure your ability to think highly of yourself and set standards of excellence in your life.

If you think big and dream big; you will create bigger decisions and generate bigger rewards, bigger payoffs and bigger incentives, bigger inspirations, and your confidence will rise in the process. Boosting your selfesteem is a key factor toward living a more successful life.

Your self-image is what will make you stand out from the average, from the timewasters, from the non-achievers, and the non-goal-oriented individuals in this big and beautiful world that we live in.

Decide on how to confront, create, challenge, and construct your standards of excellence. Take the time to think about the consequences of your actions.

What would love to accomplish in the next few days, in the next few weeks, or even the next few months? Is it a project? Is it a job offer? Do you want to travel and explore the world and change your environment? Do you want to invent the next big thing? Do you want to study, research, and learn more about new opportunities in social media?

Then decide to take action on that goal that has been a figment of your imagination, by all means necessary: set your goal, make a plan on how to achieve that goal, and implement that goal.

Whatever the case, remember, decision-making is also a key factor toward your path to a more abundant and successful life, but it is your actions that will ultimately define you. You can do this! Raise the bar, set the bar high, and capitalize, dominate, and initiate your success, for no one will do this for you. So take action, today!

8.4 Technique 4: Your Actions

Finally, nothing that you can feel and think and decide on, will amount to anything, if you cannot take action on that new idea that has been floating around in your mind for so long. You have to get those thoughts out of your head and make a plan: Write them down on paper and brainstorm or as some have called it, "Mindstorming." Take your ideas out of your head and make them a reality.

Someone once said, "The cemetery is filled with ideas and inventions that never saw the light of day," because most people never took action on their passion and they set their standards so low; they set their goals so low. They simply lived a life of mediocrity and died and never amounted to much. We will never know why but the important thing to understand is, do all you can, be all that you can be, learn all you need to know, and set high standards of excellence for yourself.

You must conjure up the courage to fulfill your destiny in life. Whatever it takes, whoever it takes talking to; network with others if possible. Do something, anything. Just take massive action, today, tomorrow, and repeat the process.

Remember, the higher the expectation, the greater the feeling you will feel deep inside your body and mind, and the greater the reward and satisfaction upon completion.

Achieving success can become addictive; a good addiction. You will want more and more of it in your life. Remember, success attracts success. Make success a habit.

Your high expectations that you set for yourself are only the cornerstone of your true ability, so continue to think high, think big, and think smart for there is no limit to your potential.

If you are willing, look down at yourself from afar and imagine yourself where you want to be in life, how you want to live, and when you want to receive these changes in your life. Stand back, observe, seek, and execute!

Your mind will help you understand your full potential, but your actions will help you get there. John C. Maxwell asserts in his book, *The 15 Invaluable Laws of Growth*, "Motivation will help you get going, but disciple will keep you growing." For us to continue growing in life, we need to discipline ourselves to do what is necessary to succeed in all aspects of our lives. Take action one step at a time, one idea at a time, one goal at a time, and if you have to— sacrifice the time needed to fulfill your mission. You can do this!

8.5 Summary and Execution

1. Never think low, always think high; exceed normality; achieve what you think is not possible.
2. Never let anyone tell you that you cannot achieve anything, not even me, because anything is possible.
3. Decide to become emotionally in control of your thoughts on a daily basis. Decide to plan a year ahead, a blueprint or a roadmap for your goals.
4. Focus on what you really want in life, and do everything in your power to get it on a daily basis. All successful leaders always have one major goal in their minds at all times: They think about what they want and how to get it.
5. Learn from other successes, learn from those who have challenged themselves and have failed and succeeded. Study them and know what not to do. All leaders are readers and they learn from one another. You must engrain yourself in your field of interest and read all the necessary material, watch the seminars, attend conferences, et cetera.
6. Remember, "Motivation gets you going, but discipline keeps you growing" John C. Maxwell.
7. Finally, no one has ever found the limit of human potential. You have more potential than you could ever use in a whole lifetime. Your mission, whether you choose to accept it or not, is to discover the one skill that will help you create wealth for you and your family. Once you have discovered the #1 skill that will help you in all aspects of your life: nourish it, feed it, and use it to the best of your ability to raise your expectations and set the highest standards of excellence in your life. You can do this!

CHAPTER 9

Exercise Your Mind

> *Reading is to the mind, as exercise is to the body.*
> -Brian Tracy

An Overview

Most people want to live a good life; they train hard in the gyms and exercise weekly. But the truth is, many individuals lose sight of the fact that they are only exercising their bodies, not their mind. Exercising your body is important toward developing a healthier lifestyle, but we must exercise our mind too.

If you want to become highly successful in all aspects of your life, you must exercise your mind. Feed it every day with mental protein: read educational books in your field; practice meditating; listen to audiobooks in your car and create the "Automobile University," or download them from your phone. Many resources are digital and at your fingertips; you just need to choose the important ones that will help you develop on a personal level.

Your mind is your most powerful asset; reprogram your mind with positive thoughts and experience the immediate change in your life. You need to think successful thoughts, say positive affirmations to yourself every day, think big dreams, if you are willing, and the list can go on and on. Master your mind, master your body, master your time, and master your life because if you don't, someone will control your life for you.

9.1 Technique 1: Your Emotions

Most people are driven by their emotions and if you cannot learn to get in touch with your emotional side, you will be destined for failure. Become emotionally driven. Find your hidden potential with mental exercises. Exercise your body, but do not by any means forget to exercise your brain. Everybody has a brain, but not everyone uses it. Why? Who knows why?

Learn to deal and block out the negative attention around you, and if you can, avoid all negative situations. Negativity will impact your emotions and ultimately, your thoughts, which will conjure up mixed messages in your mind and you will make bad decisions. As a result, your actions will show it positively or negatively. Practice and practice and practice until you can control your emotions under pressure and in serious situations.

According to neuroscience and psychology research, the brain consists of an estimated 100 billion neurons. Can you imagine all the activity, all the ideas you have within you, all the power to create anything you desire and need? Repetition is the mother of all skill, so get to work as soon as possible and make reading mental protein a habit. You will thank yourself later for having done so. Remember, all leaders are readers.

In all big, important, and successful organizations across the world, business institutions cannot function without someone reading the books for the company: the finances, the quarterly earnings, the good and bad reviews, what selling and what is not selling, and so on. You get the point. Become a better reader and a better learner.

Also, look for experts that can help you and affect the way you think about your success; they can help you. In some cases, they have the necessary skills to help you flourish. Experts can even coach you, prepare you, so when you encounter bad news as we all do in life, you will not be surprised.

Earl Nightingale asserted long ago in one of his best-selling programs, "You become what you think about all the time." Change the way you think, and you will change your life forever. Nothing could be truer. Think about your success. Think about your financial freedom and take action, today!

9.2 Technique 2: Your Thoughts

Millions of people are illiterate, others are aliterate and choose not to read. To become a high-performance individual in your field of choice, you must read all the necessary material. It is said and we repeat, "Leaders are readers." Exercise the mind and you will exercise your success. Exercise your success and you will exercise your self-esteem. You will grow and mature and feel better and prouder about yourself.

When we are doing something meaningful and purposeful, we feel good in the process; as a result, we want to repeat the process. Eventually, thinking only positive thoughts and learning how to quickly push the negative ones out of your mind, will become automatic. Too many people linger in depression, in sadness, in madness, and in complete solitude over the same negative thoughts that poison the mind. You are not one of those people.

Instead, think about being successful most of the time, visualize yourself already in possession of what you want out of life, where you want to be in 3 months, 6 months, or even many years ahead. All successful people only think about what they want and how to get it. We must mimic this mindset. Remember, nothing you are learning here is new, for all the principles and skills to become successful have been used and reused again and again.

So think about how you are going to get what you want, why you want to be successful, and what do you have to do to gain financial freedom. It has been stated as the "Law of Attraction." If you think positive things and ideas, you will attract positive people and innovative individuals. But if you think negativity, you will attract unconstructive behavior and people.

The ability to think positively no matter what happens in your life, this technique alone will change your mindset and your life forever—if—you exercise your mind as you do your body. Make your days purposeful and do not waste your time thinking about things that you cannot change.

There are many techniques to empower your mind, to empower your daily routines, to navigate your life toward an abundance of success, but you must first discipline yourself to exercise your mind in the company of your body—simultaneously. Jim Rohn once said, "You cannot change your destination overnight, but you can change your direction overnight." Take control of your life, today by taking control of your mind, today!

9.3 Technique 3: Your Decisions

Decide to get in touch with yourself, so you may reach your full potential. Most people decide that living on welfare and living an average life is normal because that is how they were trained to live, to see, and to think. They only saw successful people on TV or in a movie or now on the internet and being successful seems overwhelming. However, as the times are changing, more and more self-made millionaires are sprouting across the world because of the access and the resources available to them.

So do not be discouraged. Instead, decide to exercise and control your mind to only think about what you want, how to get it, and where do you need to go to get closer to achieving your goals. Only then will you be on the right path toward a more blissful and intelligent and prosperous life—and—a more successful life in all respects.

To continue, precision decision-making will be the key that will open doors for you. But you must encapsulate your mind with only the material and necessities that will enrich your life, not bring you down. You want to grow, and to grow, you must change; and to change, you must reprogram your mind. What you see, feel, hear, eat, and learn will ultimately define your future success.

Examine other successful people and understand their physical and mental exercises. Examine the bad and the good decisions that highly successful people made in their life at one point or another. Learn from their mistakes; learn from your mistakes, and decide to take the time every week, every month, and every year to reflect on your past achievements and failures; this technique can help tremendously.

Discipline yourself to reflect on life, on your family, on your work, and anything else that is of importance to you while you are pursuing happiness and the financial freedom you so much deserve. If we can do it, you can do it. Anybody can do it. We just must remain strong-minded and be disciplined enough to exercise our body, mind, and soul.

Not one successful entrepreneur before you—lived a life without incorporating physical and mental exercises into their daily routines. So, take action, today, and reap the rewards of positive, purposeful, physical, and mental exercises. You can do this!

9.4 Technique 4: Your Actions

Finally, plain and simple, you need to take action on your aspirations and your plans. You must realize the importance of physical and mental exercises and incorporate them into your daily schedules. High-performance driven individuals feed off of others' success, but also, they empower themselves by daily positive affirmations, taking action every day, sticking to their routines, and always asking questions.

Remain curious and ask questions like a child. Always ask questions to be more informed, to be a student, to be a good learner and a good reader. A person without questions is a person without curiosity. Questions make us think harder. Questions create new ideas, inventions, and endless opportunities for all of us. Guaranteed, where there is a success, lies a madman or woman asking millions of questions.

Remember, "Motivation will get you going, but discipline will keep you growing" John C. Maxwell. Motivate yourself by all means necessary and enrich your mind and soul with daily exercises and you will experience the difference and the positive shift in your life. Not to mention, your peers will notice your significant change of lifestyle and you will gain more positive attention and opportunities as well.

Overall, the #1 asset and tool in your arsenal, is your mind. Control your mental state and control your life, if not, someone will control it for you. Think positive, think positive thoughts and you will make positive decisions, and from that, you will execute positive actions. You can do this!

Millions of people on a daily basis do not read and enrich their current situation. Do not be placed in this category. Be a game-changer, make a better life for yourself, empower yourself by learning the necessary skills that will help you raise your expectations even higher. Do not settle for an average life or you will be considered as an average individual and you will receive an average income. Instead, become an extraordinary individual and receive extraordinary benefits and success.

If you are reading this book, this means you want to strengthen your current situation and reach your full potential. Remember, "Leaders are readers." Never stop dreaming, never let anyone tell you—you cannot succeed, or you will not succeed.

Never quit when adversities arise, never quit on your dreams. Start now. Take action, now! What do you have to lose? Take a chance and watch your life change one day at a time, one book at a time, one seminar at a time, one mentor at a time, and one exercise at a time. Continue to believe that "What the mind can conceive and believe, the mind can achieve" Napoleon Hill. If you can think it, imagine it, and feel it, whatever "it" is, in the deepest depths in your heart, you can achieve it with consistency, dedication, perseverance, and self-discipline.

9.5 Summary and Execution

1. Exercise your mind as you would exercise your body by reading beneficial books in your field of interest; Read and absorb mental protein at least 30 minutes a day.
2. Take time to meditate because your mind is your most powerful asset. And the way you use your mind, the way you feed it, creates success. You must sustain a healthy mind and body to succeed.
3. The ability to self-reflect on your past achievements and your past failures is a great technique to use when creating new successes. Learn from your mistakes, as well as, your achievements.
4. "You become what you think about most of the time." So only think about positive information and learn how to isolate and quickly replace negative thoughts with productive and positive thoughts.
5. Always think about what you want and how to get it. Always have a major goal in your life.
6. It is known as "The Law of Attraction" the more you subconsciously think about your success, the more you visualize your goals, the more chances you have of attracting people and situations and things that will help you achieve your success that you desire.
7. Finally, "All leaders are readers." If you want to become more successful than you already are, then become a better reader; become a better learner because all highly successful individuals are readers: they read books, articles, reports, and other materials from their field of interest.

CHAPTER 10

Fail and Succeed

An Overview

Every successful person and organization has failed. The steel industry, the automotive industry that designs, developments, and manufactures, the fashion industry and the retail industry; the restaurant industry, the grocery store industry, the tech industry, and just about every small business and transnational company across the globe, just to name a few—have failed before they gained momentum, stability, and profits. In truth, all industries, as of today, continue to fail.

But the only difference is, these large businesses experiment, try to provide the service and/or product that their customers want, maybe fail in the process, but they know how to bounce back from failure and adversities. These businesses simply try and try again—until they get it right, until they give the consumer something new and fresh again, and they start all over—again. Remember, repetition is the mother of all skills.

You must also experiment with your ideas, your passion, and refine your personal skills. Remember, if you never failed at anything, you never did anything. Thomas Edison once said, "I have not failed. I've just found 10,000 ways that won't work." No matter what happens, understand that failures are a part of life and we cannot control life; we can only adapt to it, adapt to life during the hard times and the good times. Be a leader and a student and learn from your failures and success.

You must challenge yourself with new opportunities constantly. Always try to surpass your expectations, and if you fail, get back up. The #1 problem in this world is: Many people fail or face hardships in their life and never reach their full potential because they accept failure and never try again. We must never fall into this category. Become strong-minded and strong-willed and engrain the possibility of failure and success.

Please, never shy away from your aspirations. You can do anything you set your mind to. Like Nike quotes, "Just Do It." So, do it once, do it twice, or do it three times; do what you must—as many times as it takes; experiment with your ideas, experiment with your life and overcome adversities and hardships. Plan accordingly and envision failures before they happen and expect them to happen, learn from them, and make the necessary changes in your life. This technique will help you conquer success in all aspects of your life.

10.1 Technique 1: Your Emotions

With billions of people on this planet, imagine all the ideas and inventions, and all the new creations that are being brought to life as you read or listen to this audiobook. If you choose to do anything, be courageous, act on your gut feeling, become emotionally charged when you have a new idea, but do not fear failure; instead, embrace it.

Someone once said, "Failure is success in the making." The world would not be what it is today if it was not for the past failures of great individuals who tried to make the world a better place. Remember this, everyone fails before they succeed; we all fail, we all are human, but we have the will, the imagination, the resources, and the intelligence to get back up and fight another day.

You need not reinvent the wheel. Everything, for the most part, has been created or duplicated and recreated again. Think about all the fiction and non-fiction books that have been written since the beginning of time. The same concepts and plots and structures remain the same across all book genres: love, murder, mystery, science fiction, children's books, self-help books, and the list can go on and on.

The point here is, do not be discouraged to proceed to the next level toward your personal and financial goals. You are not reinventing the wheel; you are giving your own spin on a past idea with a fresh new voice that will impact the lives of others, and if you are successful, you will recreate history in the process. Strengthen your emotions and recreate history; for yesterday is history. Do something today that will impact your future and do it, now!

10.2 Technique 2: Your Thoughts

Some experts estimate that the mind thinks between 60,000 to 80,000 thoughts a day. Divide that number into hours, minutes, and seconds and be astonished by how much brain cellular activity is functioning at all times in your mind. So if you want to become successful in this world, experiment—write your goals down in a notepad or type them into a computer and save your ideas, save your thoughts, and just maybe, that one idea you decide to jot down somewhere is the idea that will change your life forever.

Capture your ideas and write them down somewhere because if you do not, they will disappear like dust in the wind. Millions of people do not use this technique to capture their ideas; instead, they skip this vital step toward their success, and they simply disregard the importance of writing down their ideas. Write your ideas down and keep track of them, create a file for them, and reflect on them occasionally. It sounds so simple, yet, many individuals fail to do so and skip this vital action.

Writing down your ideas, your goals or your progress and plans in becoming successful, is a great technique to acquire to personally develop your thoughts. Experimenting with one idea may lead to another. Your thoughts swim around in your head, if you are willing, they can become a reality too. The pure action of writing down your thoughts—creates a neurological change in your body and after repetition, helps memory retention.

It is important to mention, writing down your thoughts creates your subconscious thoughts to remain active in your mind without recollection. Pretty cool. Control your experimental thoughts and control your failures and watch as you succeed in accomplishing your new ideas. Think about failure as trial and error and proceed accordingly.

Remember, you can fail and succeed in all aspects of your life, but it is your ambitious personality, your attitude toward life, and the will to experiment, fail, and succeed every day that ultimately defines you.

10.3 Technique 3: Your Decisions

Everyone wants to be successful, to be rich, others want to be famous, some want to change the world, some people want to end poverty in the world, but not everyone gets what they want. To live a more purposeful and meaningful life, you must decide what it is you really want in your life and think of how to get what you want.

Once you have decided to take the necessary steps on your thoughts and ideas, absorb and accept the fact that failure will occur during your journey and during the process of becoming a successful individual.

Become more resourceful, for the amounts of resources that are available to you, are infinite. The mentors and people you will need to succeed in life, either have written down what they have accomplished, talked about their experiences in seminars and conferences, so all you need to do is find them and decide to take action. Read their stories; listen to their failures, watch all you can watch in your field of interest. Decide what is important and block out the rest.

You have the power to choose the thoughts that linger in your mind. Decide to take the time to learn from those who have gone before you and failed and succeeded and failed again and succeeded again. Go out into the world and make your mark; you have a purpose in this world, but you just have to decide to figure out what that purpose is and experiment with it and take action on it and reinvent history.

Remember, as my professor once said, "Do what you have to do, today because yesterday is history." Make history, rewrite it, capture it, capture your ideas, initiate success, and change the way you think about what you think.

So, learn from those successful individuals who have failed and succeeded before you. Learn from those who have risen from adversities and hardships, before you.

Decide to study and research from those who you want to be inspired by. Someone once said, "Success leaves clues." Decide to follow the trail of success, not the trail of tears and fears. Be strong, be brave, be yourself, and if anything, think successful thoughts.

You deserve to be all you can be and much more. Decide to reach your full potential by studying those who have already endured and have already experienced failure; learn from them and take action on your ideas. You can do this one step at a time, one day at a time, one year at a time, but do something, anything that will change your life positively and experience the satisfaction of knowing what you want and how to get it. Now, all you have to do is, take action, today!

10.4 Technique 4: Your Actions

Finally, the fact is, most people never take action on their goals, write down their goals, or they never try to achieve their goals and gain prosperity. Do not be placed in this category or you be just another average person. All high-performance thinkers act on their decisions while average people, if ever, never regain the courage to get back up and try again after failure. Fail once, fail twice, or even fail three times; no matter how many times you fail, get up with your head held high.

Thomas Edison failed 999 times before he created the light bulb. The truth is, there is no success in life without experiencing some sort of failure. We learn from our mistakes, we learn from our shortcomings, and we should examine our past, not live in it, but reevaluate the past and move on quickly: use this, gain momentum and keep moving forward. Always move forward and never backward.

Remember, all your actions will be short-term decisions, but they will have long-term rewards. You may fail at times, but the courage to overcome them, learn from them, and recreate another more purposeful outcome, will make all the difference in the end and create positive results.

In the end, it is knowing how to emotionally and mentally accept, learn, study, and educate yourself . . . that will ultimately define you and your future success in all aspects of your life. All game-changers, winners, entrepreneurs, and everyone successful before you have experienced failure one time or another in their lifetime. Be smart and mentally strong and take action, today!

10.5 Summary and Execution

1. Try to envision success no matter what happens, no matter what people say, no matter the difficulties placed in your path as you try to achieve your goals.

2. Most people never set goals for themselves. Do not fall into this category. Live your passion, live your life to the fullest, and always try new things and you will be rewarded for your efforts and determination and your insatiable desire to succeed.

3. Experiment and fail if necessary, but fail quickly and get back up and succeed swiftly. Do not linger in the past for too long. We must learn from our failures, our mishaps, and our difficulties that are placed in our path, learn all we can while we can.

4. Educate yourself in the process of failing: evaluate failure; study it, and reflect on it. This technique will help you mature physically and mentally.

5. Every successful organization has failed. Products and services morph into another product or service.

6. Innovation and success are a world full of failures, but keep trying at everything that you are passionate about and you will eventually succeed.

7. The law of attraction says that you will become what you desire in life if you can hold that desire in your mind long enough; if you can believe positively every day; if you live an energized life every week; and if you can hold your ideas and goals in your mind indefinitely without distraction, you will succeed inevitably. Say this to yourself every day, "Success for me is inevitable!" and it will be so.

CHAPTER 11

First Impressions

An Overview

There is one thing you can do that can help you look and feel successful, it is to dress for success every day. Dress as if you are wealthy and successful. Dress like a professional. "Dress to impress." Your wardrobe is the first thing people will see aside from your face. The mere fact of dressing nice and looking clean will boost your self-esteem, people will compliment you. You will gain more attention, opportunities, and respect.

First impressions are so important because your image will leave either a bad or a wonderful memory toward your audience—whoever they may be. Everyone has their reasons to dress the part, look the part, but we must look sharp, clean, and presentable in order to influence others. Remember, you will feel more confident when you are walking into an interview dressed for the occasion, rather than wearing anything that is readily available to you. Dressing for success is not only important in your professional and business life, but also in your personal life; experience the difference when you look amazing, sharp, and clean.

If you want to work somewhere in specific, take the time to research a bit. Review your environment, the people where you want to work, the boss and the employees, and if you can, keenly observe how they dress. It is important to not wear a suit if no one in the organization will be wearing one, especially, in an interview. Look the part. Do not oversimplify the moment. Take charge of your life.

For example, a person interviewing for a vice president position will wear a suit while a person interviewing to be a cook in a restaurant will not wear one; he or she will be overdressed and maybe, considered as overqualified. Take the time to research and dress for success because the first impression may be your last impression. Make your presence known and it will pay off in the end.

11.1 Technique 1: Your Emotions

Millions of people dress casually or wear anything that makes them feel comfortable. You must dress as if you already own a business, as if you are an entrepreneur, and as if you already have millions of dollars. This technique may sound silly, but what you wear—will make you feel confident and attractive. Your clothing and the way you carry yourself will also boost your self-image.

Dressing for success at all times will help you become self-aware of your self-image. You will not only feel important and attractive, but you will also gain the attention of others in the process. The law of attraction will be working for you without you even knowing. Remember, you must attract success and vice-versa.

Begin to dress, walk, and feel more confident daily and experience the impact it will leave on your peers, friends, and your co-workers. You will feel more excited on a daily basis and therefore, raise your expectations, and inevitably, want more out of life. We all want more, and we all deserve more.

But the point and the fact here is, if you want to climb the ladder of success, you need to look the part, dress accordingly and be willing to change, and transform your lifestyle and the way of living in the process. You can do this.

11.2 Technique 2: Your Thoughts

Unfortunately, many people do not take the necessary time to think about how their wardrobe impacts them: their personal development, their future, or their chance at landing their next dream job. Aside from having a great personality and a skillset, you need to think hard about the long-term effect your dress-ethic will leave on your intended audience.

Whether you are making a video, conducting a seminar on the internet, or meeting someone in person, think about how your self-image is going to impact them and their friends. Do you want your presence to be positive, negative, or neither? Take charge of your life and think about wealth, success, and the way you dress; the results will be astounding and long-lasting.

Only you can make the choice. Unleash your inner you and always dress for success, but first, always think of who you want to impress. Whomever that may be—a woman or a man, a professional or a person at a casual party, maybe a person in a business meeting or a family member at a family reunion, no matter the time of day or the individual, you have the power to look fancy or look average and simple.

Remember, what people see on the outside does impact what they feel on the inside. Create a spontaneous, successful and attractive future, but more importantly, an everlasting one—just by simply dressing for success. A memorable first impression may be all you need toward your next step in becoming an inspirational, motivational, and successful individual. Decide and change the way you dress and carry yourself, today, if you have not already.

11.3 Technique 3: Your Decisions

Decide where you want to work. Look at how the people dress there. Mimic their wardrobe and dress accordingly. You can gain a person's trust by simply getting on their level. If you want to work at a bank, dress like them. If you want to work on wall-street, dress like a stockbroker. If you want to be an athlete, dress like one.

The point is: until you decide on the career path that you want to take in life, you will not be able to dress for the part. But until then, decide to wear clothes that make you look as if you are a wealthy individual. You have nothing to lose, but everything to gain by looking your best at all times.

Regardless, gaining momentum is the next step toward building your self-image, becoming more self-confident, and ultimately, gaining the attention of the superiors from various organizations that you desire to work for. Your decision to dress for success will ultimately define you. Take action, today and experience positive results!

11.4 Technique 4: Your Actions

Finally, the mere act of slipping on clothes that fit you properly can look appealing not only to you but to others. Dressing up for a gathering at one of your friend's houses, dressing up for a meeting in downtown, or dressing up for a vacation with a partner of your choice, are just a few examples of places you can go, and you will never know who you will run into.

In this day and age, a business opportunity, a new prospect, or a new networking opportunity could be right in front of you.

Taking action on grooming themselves is what millions of people fail to do every day. Some fail to do so, and some do not. Some succeed and some do not. Who knows why? We do not know why, but the important thing to understand is, we must take action on how we carry ourselves every day. Rise above the average people and seek more of your self-image and always look your best. Always dress your best.

Take the time to be clean and dress for success and observe how others around you notice you and compliment you and notice how they treat you. You may be astonished by the results. Maybe it will be your partner, maybe a friend, maybe a colleague, maybe a client, or whomever it may be, the reward is uplifting and a boost to your self-esteem. Reap the rewards intentionally not accidentally.

The chances of you living a more successful life will be in your favor, and you will gain a sense of satisfaction. Eventually, you will want to repeat the feeling of being complimented and respected by others. Wearing nice clothes that fit you properly will not only become a habit but normal. In time, you will never leave your home without dressing for success.

Take action, today, for yesterday is history. Make your next first impression memorable and remarkable, and thank yourself later for taking the time to look your best. You will not regret ever taking the time to dress for success. You can do this. We only live once, so dress for success, and succeed to the fullest and reach your full potential.

11.5 Summary and Execution

1. Always look your best: dress sharp, groom yourself, and the payoff will be grand.
2. Always research the job you want and dress accordingly; for example, if you want to work on wall street, wear a suit, if you want to work in a restaurant, dress casual.
3. Wear clothes that fit you, not that hang off your bottom and that are baggy and raggedy. Always look like a professional individual—if that is what you are striving for. Bottom line, dress to impress!
4. Dress as if you are already a millionaire, a person of importance. This technique will boost your selfesteem, gain more positive attention, people will respect you more, and more financial opportunities may arise by simply dressing clean.
5. Preparation is the key to your success: look like a bum and you will get paid like one. Look like a million bucks and you will be rewarded.
6. The truth is, people, see you first on the outside before they get to know you on the inside. First impressions are exceptional, important and can be long-lasting, memorable, and remarkable. So "Dress for Success."
7. In your personal life, in your professional life, and your private life, dress to impress, dress casually, and always dress accordingly. You will feel better and you will look better. Take charge of your life and "Dress to Impress and Nothing Less."

CHAPTER 12

Visualize Your Success

An Overview

The power of visualization is within us all. Many people live but do not use this inner power. You must visualize yourself already successful. Imagine you already own a big, beautiful house, a large property, you are working and doing what you love, you have a healthy and beautiful family, and envision your financial freedom. The list can go on and on.

Envisioning yourself wealthy will encourage you and drive you toward accomplishing your goals. Seeing yourself in a position of power, is more powerful than seeing yourself in a position of poverty. This technique will help you push you in the direction you desire. Which direction do you want to go in?

Though, you may not have everything you want—yet.

The fact is, you are implanting the success thoughts in your mind, which will help you make better decisions toward achieving ultimate success and getting what you want. There will be obstacles and people will try to hinder you from reaching your full potential, but keep moving; keep striving for what you want; keep studying and visualizing your success. For that reason, do not unveil all your aspirations to everyone, but continue to envision yourself successful and take control of your mind.

The power of visualizing yourself successful is a technique that can have a grand and positive effect on your future. Give it a try and experience the change that will occur in your life.

12.1 Technique 1: Your Emotions

Have you ever wanted something to the point that you will do anything to get it? Have you wanted to do something in your life or go somewhere, and you do everything in your power to achieve this short-term goal of yours?

These emotions were created by the mere fact that you are visualizing yourself in control; you are already there, and you are already in possession of what you want. You just do not have it yet. Some people say it is a premonition, or that you are psychic. In reality, you create and see your own destiny by visualizing what you want and by taking action on that vision. Eventually, you push yourself to the point of success, and you get what you want by any means necessary.

We all wanted to walk, and we did. We all wanted to drive, and we did. We all wanted to do something or wanted something in life, and we got it. We just have to use that same power within us to get all that we need and want and desire to be more successful. Visualizing your goals will help you get there quicker.

You must not underestimate the power you have within your mind. If you can imagine, if you can dream, if you can feel, if you can touch, if you can hear, if you can taste, and if you are willing to sacrifice and take the time to visualize yourself already being successful, you will get everything you want in life.

The fact that you can visualize yourself finishing a task at work, or finishing a chore at home or anywhere for that matter, should be motivation to push you toward achieving and stretching your goals further. Learn, envision, and harness this technique, and you will realize how powerful and beneficial the outcomes in your life will amount to in the end.

Some experts say, "Achieving your goals is 75% psychological and 25% mechanics." In other words, three-fourths of what you think about will have a grander impact, than the twenty-five percent of mechanics that you will incorporate into achieving that goal. Master your mind, master your emotions, and change the way you live your life, but more importantly, take control of your life by planning and visualizing your next move. Do it, now!

Envision your success; envision yourself already equipped with the necessary skills that can help you succeed; and envision your potential opportunities that may change your life. Use your emotional powers to envision your life with the end in mind as the American educator, Stephen Covey mentioned long ago.

12.2 Technique 2: Your Thoughts

If you can do anything, take the time to find a quiet environment where you can get in touch with the power of visualization. Once you have successfully learned to connect with your consciousness and your deepest inner thoughts, only then, will you truly understand what you want out of life, how to get it, and what it is that is stopping you from getting what you desire; this technique (The Power of Visualization) will help you.

Control your thoughts to only think about what you want, not what you do not want. Clarity and focus are the keys to our successes in all aspects of our lives.

Make it a habit to see yourself successful in the present and in the future, and if you are willing and persistent, make it a reality. Your thoughts will control your deepest decisions, desires and your subconscious, and your decisions will ultimately control your actions. You will accomplish what you thought was never possible. You will begin to encounter opportunities and meet new people who want to succeed in life too. This is the secret of "The law of Attraction." You will attract what you think about most of the time.

Obstacles may still hinder you, but the fact is, the ability to visualize what you want, can play a critical role in your future success. Eventually, your mind will overlook and overpower the difficulties in front of you and only focus on the positive visualizations that you have implanted in your mind.

We all have negative thoughts that arise in our minds. But knowing how to replace these thoughts with positive ones, positive visualizations, and positive affirmations, will ultimately, determine the speedy change toward a more prosperous and successful life.

Some of the greatest minds of all time have used the power of visualization: artists, statesman, athletes, entrepreneurs, and students, just to name a few. The fact is, knowing what you want, why you want it, and where you want to go in life, can be your roadmap to financial freedom. The power of visualizing yourself already successful is an essential tool in your arsenal to combat the negativity that you do not need nor want in your life. You can do this!

12.3 Technique 3: Your Decisions

Decide to find a place and practice the art of visualization. Visualizing something in your mind can have a long-term effect. Decide only to watch and read positive material that will only help you in achieving your goals in life. Someone once said, "As long as you are focused on your inner-goals, you will achieve success." Visuals are everywhere, but choosing what to record in your mind will be the ultimate challenge and the bridge between success and stagnation.

Therefore, decide to block out the negativity and visualize only success and successful people, successful stories, positive testimonials and visualize opportunities. Flood your mind with nothing but positivity and watch as your goal-oriented visualizations come to life before you. The reward will be bountiful. Take action, today!

12.4 Technique 4: Your Actions

Finally, the moment of truth. Once you visualize yourself in possession of what you want, you have to act on that thought. Without holding back, your actions will spur more creativity and you will attempt to reach your full potential. Push yourself, discipline yourself, and fight for what you want. Do what is needed to get what you seek in life.

Many people never even try to pursue their dreams because they fear what is not a reality. Do not fear anything; create your dreams and make them a reality one day at a time. Choose success over poverty. Choose financial independence over living in poverty. Choose to live your dreams without fear.

Do not be clouded by fear or by what others will tell you, just do what you feel is right, and ultimately, you will achieve greatness, you will reach your intended destination, and only then, will you possess and have total control of what you thought was never possible.

The joy of visualization is simple, clear, and the power is in your mind, and only you can see what others cannot. And only you can act on that visual that you have in your mind. So take action and attempt to visualize your future success. Experience the impact and the power of your own mind. Only you can take action on your visualizations. Do it, now! You can do this.

12.5 Summary and Execution

1. Visualization is a technique that can help you, guide you, and push you toward seeing what you desire. Take the time to visualize yourself successful.
2. Many people never use the power of visualization. Visualize yourself in possession of what you want.
3. Visuals are all around us. What you choose to focus your attention on will be the determiner of your future success. Choose only to focus on success principles, success stories every day. Your mind is more powerful than anything in this world.
4. The ultimate challenge is to not be clouded by other people's goals and visuals. Discipline yourself to control your deepest desires in life. Engrain only positive material into your subconscious mind.
5. Fortify your mind from negativity, negative people, and negative visuals for this will hinder you and slow you down from achieving your goals.
6. The power of visualization is so powerful that once you learn how it works and how to use it, you will never stop using it again. You can use it on a test in school, on a fitness goal, a financial goal, a health or wealth goal, or anything that you desire. Use It!
7. The power of visualization works by "The law of Attraction" simply because, you will attract what you are thinking about most of the time. Visualize poverty and you will only think about poverty issues and things of that nature. Think about successful people and success opportunities and the principles of success; then, you will want to study them. Choose the lifestyle you want to live, people you want to meet, goals you want to achieve, today!

CHAPTER 13

Self-Education is Vital

> *Books are what you step on to take you to a higher shelf.
> The higher your stack of books, the higher the shelf you can
> reach. Want to reach higher? Stack some more books under
> your feet! Reading is what brings us to new knowledge. It
> opens new doors. It helps us understand mysteries. It lets
> us hear from successful people. Reading is what takes us
> down the road in our journey. Everything you need for a
> better future and success has already been written.*
>
> -Jim Rohn

An Overview

Millions of people across the world have had some form of education—either at home, in school, private or public. Whatever the case may be, you must never stop learning new things. Never stop learning in your field of interest. Never stop reading material that will enrich your mind with new ideas and concepts for the future. Knowledge rapidly changes, so you must stay up-to-date with the current information, the current trend, and the current data in your field of interest.

It has been stated, "Knowledge is power," but this is not true, "knowledge is only potential power; execution will trump knowledge any day" (Tony Robbins). Your ability to know what information will empower you, will be the overall key to your success. Continue to study and educate yourself. Master your skill, master your craft, master your passion, master your goals; master your life and raise your expectations and execute.

Warren Buffet once said, "The more you learn, the more you earn." Put your knowledge to good use and help others if you can. The more you know, the more you grow. The more you know, the smarter you are. The smarter you are, the more influential you will be. Inevitably, you will be able to communicate with more people and extend your knowledge.

However, you cannot learn everything in life. But by taking in only the necessary knowledge you crave and need, you will stretch your mind, exceed your mental capacity, and you will increase your brain function and live a long and healthy life. Remember, leaders are readers, so never stop reading and taking in new knowledge and learning new things.

13.1 Technique 1: Your Emotions

Educating yourself is so important to your emotional state of mind. Feeding your mind with mental protein is essential to the next step in climbing the ladder of success as many have before you. Knowledge is all around you; can you feel it?

Emotionally, every city is packed with knowledge. Look around you right now; take the time to feel your environment, your home, your vehicle, the streets, the land and place where we stand and live. Long ago, someone once felt that building and creating a city would be a good idea, so they decided to build one.

The way you interpret knowledge and use it will ultimately define you. Build your success; build your dreams, build your ideas one small piece at a time.

If you feel something inside you, a gut feeling to want to do something that might change your reality or someone else's, then do it. You have nothing to lose.

Your idea will never come to reality if you do not act on that feeling. Yes, you must educate yourself more, but you should also take action and execute your knowledgeable thoughts. If not, someone else will act on their thoughts and ideas. The world is full of ideas, so build the confidence to succeed in all aspects of your life. You can do this.

Never stop believing in yourself, never stop learning, and never stop executing new ideas. If you fail, try again and again and again. You will gain momentum, and in time, your efforts will pay off. Remember, if you never failed at anything, you never did anything in life. Educate yourself more and experience the grand effect that it will have on you toward becoming a more successful individual and living a more purposeful life. Never give up.

13.2 Technique 2: Your Thoughts

All successful individuals think about what they want and how to get it. So, the ability to think constantly about what you want and how to get it, is a clue that you are thinking like a successful individual and that you are on the right track. But, you want more. You need more. You know you deserve more. Your family deserves more. You deserve greatness.

So educate yourself more every day, think and repeat positive affirmations on a daily basis. Become more resourceful. Because when you have more resources at your disposal, you will be introduced to other people's knowledge and you will learn from those intelligent individuals who have experienced failure and success.

Think and act rich, and you will become wealthy and successful. Think and act poor, and you will always live a life of poverty. Choose to learn more, to want more, and to educate yourself more and you will want more in your life. Continue to create a rich-thinking mentality. Continue to maintain a strong, intelligent mindset. Think like a highly successful person and you will inevitably become a highly success-driven individual and become unstoppable.

To choose to think and never stop learning, is a wonderful technique you can add to your arsenal for living a more abundant and successful life. Also, people will respect you more; as a result, you will highly increase your chances for more profitable opportunities.

13.3 Technique 3: Your Decisions

If you decide to educate yourself more, not only will you be noticed by your superiors, more advancements will arise. Chances for a promotion, new opportunities and avenues will appear before you. Decide to study at least a few times a week.

"We all have the same 24 hours in a day, but what you do with those 24 hours will change your life forever" (Brian Tracy). You can make more money, but you cannot recreate extra time. What will you do with your 24 hours? What can you decide to do or not do that will benefit you, right now? Decide to think like a leader and take charge of your life like a champion.

If you are willing, set aside the necessary hours for reading nourishing material, which will help you succeed toward your goals and aspirations. There is a time for work; there is a time for recreation; there is a time for family; there is a time for vacation, but if you want to rise from obscurity and poverty, you must set aside the necessary time for self-education and the execution of all your goals.

Execute your knowledge and make a difference in this world once you have acquired the necessary and fundamental skills to succeed in life. Because we live in the wealthiest and most prosperous nation in the world, there is no excuse to not succeed if you decide you want to.

"Everything you need for a better future and success has already been written" (Jim Rohn). Success is learnable, teachable, and more accessible than any other time in history. Now, you cannot learn everything, but learn all that you need to know to become a leader in your field of interest. Believe in yourself and educate yourself and reap the benefits of your hard work. You can do this!

13.4 Technique 4: Your Actions

Finally, what will you do once you have acquired the fundamental knowledge and the personal skills you desire? What will you do with that knowledge? Will you write a book, present a talk on a show, create an informative webinar, teach others on the internet, or try to influence others and change the world?

There are many options for you. The secret is: The more you teach others what you know, the more you ingrain and retain all that you have learned throughout your educational journey. If you do not execute—your knowledge will cease to exist, and your chances for living a successful life will decline tremendously. It cannot be said enough, "You either use it or lose it."

In the end, it is our ability to take action and execute immediately that defines us. We must never stop learning new things. Execution is important toward your professional and personal development: your entrepreneur endeavors, your ideas, your decision to manage your time more effectively, your decision to think only about what you want out of life, on educating yourself daily; execution, execution, and more execution on all your facets of your life, is the number one key to all your successes.

Begin to execute and achieve success because you and your family deserve it. Take action, today, and experience the difference when you take the time to enhance your personal and professional development with the power of self-education and execution. You can do this!

13.5 Summary and Execution

1. Never stop learning new things in life; continue to sharpen your personal and professional skills.
2. The more you learn the more you earn, so get to work immediately on your craft. Remember, time and the years are going to pass anyway.
3. "Knowledge is only potential power" but the ability to execute and continue to take massive action on all that you are learning will be the determiner of your success.
4. Do not take your intelligence for granted because if you do not use it, you lose it! Plain and simple, if you gain new knowledge, you must use it effectively, daily, and consistently to master your craft and *Develop A Genius Mindset*.
5. Dominate and execute by all means necessary. Single out all negative material and people out of your lives and only decide to take action and take in positive and construct material that will enrichen your life, move you toward your goals, and ultimately, boost your self-esteem.
6. New information is always being created, being developed, and brought into the mainstream for public and private ventures. Do not fall behind; instead, transform your life with new knowledge.
7. Try to get on the same frequency that other successful people in your field of interest are on. Connect and seek their advice. Self-education is the key to success. Communicate and educate yourself by all means necessary: read the books or listen to the audiobooks; watch the seminars; attend the conferences, but do not give up, for eventually, you will meet the right people that will guide you and your talents to the next level of success that you desire.

CHAPTER 14

Maintain a Rich Mindset

—❝——

When you change the way you look at things, the things you look at—change.

-Wayne Dyer

——❞—

An Overview

Many people feel as if their current situation will never change because they have a negative mindset. A negative way of thinking will limit your potential. You will only feel, see, and believe all the negativity and failures within the world around you, rather than beauty and success that lingers beneath the surface.

You must not be placed in this category of people, for you—yourself will never change, or reach your full potential. You must see the good in all things. Think as if everything that is happening around you is an opportunity for you to change and better your life. Use this technique and gradually your life will change. Believe in your ideas when you have one and act on it quickly.

Your mindset will guide you, either to more failures and negative images; or, toward a more prosperous, healthy and wealthy life—

only—if you can believe in a rich life. A rich and positive life can become a reality. Change the way you think, change the way you act, change the way you talk, change the way you see life and your way of living and your income will change forever.

Do not change who you are, only change your frame of thinking, and everything positive in your life will come into place by "the law of attraction." Take the next step toward a healthier and wealthier life by simply changing your mindset if you have not already. The outcomes will be astonishing and your payoff for doing so will be abundant.

14.1 Technique 1: Your Emotions

If you can control your emotions, you can control your destiny. The world we live in is diverse, but your ability to feel powerful and see only the positive in everything will ultimately define your future success. You must think only of what you want in life, why you want it, and how you can get it. Don't think about all the negativity in the world like people dying, for these imaginations will only encapsulate your emotions, lower your self-esteem, and distract and confuse your decision-making.

In reality, the majority of things that happen around the world cannot be changed by you alone. Many people around the world are flooded with news about deaths, war and poverty, which you have no control over. Decide to change your way of thinking from now on and become who you are destined to be. Unleash your inner creativity and think about your goals in life on a daily, weekly, and monthly basis. Take charge of your life; take charge of your emotions and experience the difference.

Focus your emotions on your aspirations and achievements, small and big. You will feel better in the end. Your body will feel better, your mind will feel relaxed. So, free yourself from all anxiety in the world. Become more focused on your goals—not everyone else's problems. You want more power, more control, more clarity, and clear thinking incorporated into your daily life, then you must take control of your emotions.

The technique of practicing to control your emotions and thinking positively and richly will ultimately change your mindset and define your success at the end of the day. You can do this!

14.2 Technique 2: Your Thoughts

Earl Nightingale asserted long ago, "You become what you think about." The more you incorporate negative images into your mind, the more drastic and uneasy and unbalanced your decision-making will become. Your thoughts are like a source of energy that will empower your future success or bring you down to a dark road of failures if you let it. We may not have control of what happens in the world, but the one greatest asset you do have control of is—your thoughts!

If you want to do something, today and change the course of your life, change the way you see and think about things in and around your environment. If you can conduct this technique every day for the next thirty days or more; eventually, your thoughts will change your frame of thinking.

Live life purposefully and positively and your attitude will become a force of habit. Eventually, the habit of thinking only of positive things and taking in only positive images into your mind will become automatic, so begin as soon as possible.

14.3 Technique 3: Your Decisions

Decide to only see rich and powerful images. Decide to think about the things that are only within your reach. Think about the things that you can only physically change. Watching positive mass media, seminars, videos, reading educational books, etc. Decide to gather with supportive family members only, trustworthy friends, or form a mastermind group that you can meet with occasionally.

Whatever the strategy that suits you, build a more solid foundation for the support of your journey toward your success and financial freedom.

The point here is, flooding your mind with positivity instead of negativity will drastically change your mindset and create a more successful, meaningful, and purposeful lifestyle. If you can think it, if you can dream it, if you can decide to do it, you can change all aspects within and around your life. With time, hard work, effort, and a positive mindset, your possibilities are endless.

14.4 Technique 4: Your Actions

Finally, take action by surrounding yourself with people smarter than you, people with bigger responsibilities than you. People who are leaders in an organization. Learn from them. Continue to change your mindset by changing who you meet with daily, weekly, or monthly basis. Dan Pena implied long ago, "Show me your friends and I'll show you your future."

If your friends are bringing you down, change them. If your colleagues are leading you nowhere in life, abandon them. And if your unsatisfied with your current situation in life, change it completely.

Take action and watch, observe keenly as your life changes; inevitably, your mindset will change, too. As a result, more opportunities will arise. Leaders will respect you more and you will gain a higher pay if you put in the hard work. You will be on your way to achieving a clearer frame of thinking, which is the most powerful asset you have.

Millions of people underestimate their ability to think. Someone once said, "The hardest thing to do is to think." Thinking and self-reflection and the ability to use your imagination can open up doors and more opportunities in your life than just living an average life. Take action quickly while your emotions are high. Do not wait for success to come to you and show up on your doorstep because it never will.

We must take action and discipline ourselves to think voraciously and accurately, clearly, and chase the opportunities. If you want something in life, you gotta go for it; go get it.

You have to be hungry and chase the riches and the wealth you desire. You have to have clarity in all your decision-making. A clear frame of thinking can unleash your inner power and ultimately, unleash your true full potential in the process. Take action and change your mindset and change your life, today. Remember, your mind is your most powerful asset, so nourish it and feed it with positive and rich content, and watch your dreams come true.

14.5 Summary and Execution

1. "You become what you think about most of the time" so only think about becoming a highly driven individual

2. If you can think it, if you can dream it; you can surely achieve it with hard work, effort and by means of using your most powerful asset, your mind.

3. If you can control your emotions, you can control your thoughts, if you can control your thoughts, you can control your decisions, and your decisions create positive or negative results. You are in control.

4. Control your mind, and you can control your life.

5. The mind is more powerful than anything else in this world, for without it, nothing in this world would be here today.

6. If you can think, you can become rich and gain financial freedom. Think of poverty and sadness and disparity and speak like that, you will live in that frame of thinking forever. But, think like a rich man, read what the wealthy read, talk and walk and learn from the successful people that have gone before us and we become successful too.

7. "Do not reinvent the wheel." Everything has already been done for you. All you have to do is: discipline yourself, maintain a strong mindset, and take action on your ideas and watch as the world changes around you.

CHAPTER 15

Success Leaves Clues

An Overview

Living life without learning from others is impossible. Remember success leaves clues; our job is to rediscover them. From the time we were children, up until our adulthood, we have judged others without even knowing we were doing it. You said he or she was funny. He looks skinny. She looks pretty. Their family is so weird. Their mom is crazy. Their dad is a drunk. The list can go on and on.

The way you interpret the lives of others will reflect your perception of yourself, your characteristics, and your actions. Think like a leader and learn to read other people's emotions, relate to their hardships, and their upbringing, and use those characteristics from everyone you encounter to communicate with your audience effectively.

Instead of only judging others, learn from them. Learn from others' weaknesses, their faults, their hardships in life. Examine and learn from the poverty and the bad conditions that people live in and why they live in those conditions. Day after day, people unconsciously create mistakes. For you to appreciate your future success, you must understand why you want to break and change your cycle of living. What is your purpose in life?

Understanding your surroundings, the communities around you, the cities around you, and the other states around you, will strengthen your ability to conquer poverty and rise from your current position in life. Be grateful and always give thanks for what you have. Appreciate life, appreciate every breath, appreciate that you are alive and healthy, and you will grow and be inspired in the process.

Receive the power to gain the success you are chasing by gaining an understanding and a self-awareness of yourself, but more importantly, an emotional intelligence of your surroundings and the people that exist within it.

15.1 Technique 1: Your Emotions

If you can learn to feel empathy for others on a personal level, you can learn to succeed at the professional level. This technique is appreciated and has been learned by all leaders from all industries across the world: from presidents, executives, business affiliates, and all other professional individuals who have studied the art of leadership and success.

The fact of the matter is, you cannot live life without seeing others as they are, but you can learn from them. You can feel their pain. You can connect with them. You can know how not to live, what not to do, and what you would never want to endure again.

You are in some way connected to everyone, we all are connected in some way or another. Become a leader in your field of interest and learn the art of emotional intelligence, a leadership quality, and learn all you can, but do not judge others; instead, use that knowledge to adapt to your surroundings accordingly.

15.2 Technique 2: Your Thoughts

The problem with many people is that they have been judged by others as stupid or mentally retarded, and they never changed their state of mind. Or, they were never encouraged to succeed. Or, they were told something negative about themselves and they never took the time to learn from others, or psychologically, they could not learn at all because they never had any proper schooling.

Some people will live the rest of their lives in this frame of thinking. You must not fall into this category. If you are blessed with the ability to think for yourself, you are already blessed to create new ideas, inventions, and build a foundation for the future of your success.

You must disregard anything any mean teacher or friend, or higher authority ever told you. Do not be discouraged any longer. Break free from a world of average thinking and into a world of global success and communication. Change your mind-set. Learn from the world around you. Learn what not to become. Learn and understand that you can better your current situation regardless of the obstacles in front of you; instead, go around them.

Study the lives of successful people. Do not forget where you came from, but crawl out of your safe-haven and change your life by taking a chance. Only you can think for yourself. Only you can decide to become successful. Learn from the poverty and the mishaps of others, and use that to your advantage. You may have lived a life of poverty too; this is your advantage and leverage, use it! We all have had discouraging parents in some cases, but we must break free and break the chains of poverty and grab the chains of success.

Do not live your life judging others because they may have judged you horribly in the past. Instead, control your thoughts, control your emotions, control your decisions, and your actions will define your future success. Someone once said, "It is not where you are from that matters, it is what you are doing and where you are going, now, that will define you." What will you become in the process of chasing your dreams and goals? Think big, dream big, and take charge of your emotions and take charge of your life, today.

15.3 Technique 3: Your Decisions

Decide to not live in the past and worry about what others thought of you at one point in your life. Everything, everyone, and everywhere you have lived has created the person you are today. You are more powerful, smarter, and more careful because of your past. Being aware of your past can strengthen your ability to connect with people. Or, deciding to live and think of the past, can weaken your ability to connect with people.

Make the decision to become self-aware of yourself and other peoples' emotions and this unique technique will help you make better decisions and communicate with other people because you have gone through the same thing they have.

Many motivational speakers use the technique of reliving their lives in a short story, and they express it to the world, so they can connect with their audience on that level. Decide to not hide who you once were, use that to fuel the fire of your success in which you seek. It has been stated, "Only God can judge you," but the truth is, only you can decide and judge the future of your success.

Be authentic. Do not let the judgments of others affect what you want out of life. Follow your dreams, follow your ambitions, and study and learn from past successes and failures. You can do this!

15.4 Technique 4: Your Actions

Finally, the most important thing of all is, taking action. Many have said, "Success leaves clues." Successful people are all around you. Get out there in the world, and you will see that many people are living lives of happiness and they are surrounded by wealth and knowledge. It is true, millions of people continue to live in poverty, but you cannot control that. You want more for you; you want more for your family and your potential grandchildren, so remain focused on your short-term and long-term goals.

Instead of worrying about what others think of you, study successful individuals: entrepreneurs and big company organizations, research current success if you can. Act now and read material from the field that interest you. Whether it be science, math, English, the fashion industry, graphic design, gaming, technology, sports, engineering, or whatever your passion is, someone has written about their failures and their rise to becoming successful in that specific subject.

So, take the time and take action, read and succeed and that is all you need. Become a life-long student, do not judge other people, but instead, learn from them, learn their culture, learn their heritage, and learn all you need to know to become more successful in your passion of study.

Hundreds, if not thousands of audiobooks, seminars, podcasts, interviews, books, just to name a few, are just some of the resources where you can act now—and study enriching material. Learn from the successful people and take advantage of the time you have now, for yesterday is history. Take action, today, and change your life forever.

15.5 Summary and Execution

1. From the time we were children we have been judging people without thinking. But times have changed, so take charge of your emotions and your thoughts and use your intellect and knowledge to connect with other people on their level.

2. All leaders learn from other people. They use the art of "emotional intelligence," the ability to have empathy for others. Instead of judging people, we must learn from each other's experiences.

3. At one point in our lives, someone fooled us, told us that we were not good enough. But the truth is, people will tell you ugly things because they will never amount to nothing. Take charge of your emotions and you will take charge of your life.

4. Everyone has a purpose in life. It has been written, "The most important days in your life are the day you were born and the day you found out why." What is your purpose in life?

5. Everything, everyone, and everywhere you have lived has created the person you are today. Break free from it, take charge of your emotions, thoughts, decisions, and your actions. If you will do this, your future success will be reachable, achievable, feasible, and attainable.

6. We all have a past, but not everyone is proud of it. Make the choice to use it or lose it, quickly!

7. All leaders learn and grow from one another. Do not be discouraged. Study success, learn and read the books, watch the necessary seminars, attend conferences, and watch the videos that will add fuel to your fire, not put it out. "Success Leaves Clues."

CHAPTER 16

Self-Discipline

—❝——

The charged life, then, usually calls to us after we have done what we were supposed to do, become who we thought we were supposed to be, lived as we thought we were supposed to live. Growth and greatness often come from those seemingly endless, fruitless days of discipline. Keep working, keep at it, believe.

-Brendon Burchard

——❞—

An Overview

The ability to discipline yourself to visualize your aspirations, your dreams, and everything you want in life, is essential and another steppingstone toward your ultimate future success. Many people fail to discipline themselves and as a result, they never achieve excellence, pursue their goals, or rise and fight their way out of obscurity and poverty.

You must discipline yourself to stay focused when distractions arise and when negative people try to hinder your thoughts. Discipline yourself to say no when needed and express yourself accordingly. Self-discipline is success in the making—one step at a time, one book at a time, one seminar at a time, one interview at a time, one video at a time, one prospect at a time.

The ability to discipline yourself right now, to do what is necessary even when you do not feel like doing it, is what will separate you from living an average or an insignificant life. Someone once said, "If you do what is hard now, you will live an easy life, but if you do what is easy now you will live a hard life." Most people choose short-term gain and they receive long-term pain. Only you can make the choice that will define you and your future success.

To have the willpower to align your life and structure your goals, accordingly, is one of the most important techniques to learn, if not, the #1 technique. Because without discipline, a person is working, living, and surviving by the means of others who are goal-oriented and self-disciplined. Someone once said, "If you do not plan your life, someone will plan it for you."

The point here is, plan, learn, and discipline yourself to set mental triggers, to visualize your opportunities; learn to use your full power and take control of your mind. Use your mental powers to dominate and get what you want in life. Master your mind, master your life, discipline yourself, and change your life forever.

You may be self-disciplined, but you are subconsciously unaware of it. Discover your inner-power and take charge of your life, today! Explore and identify your boundaries, seize the day, seize the week, seize the month, seize the year and watch, observe, and evaluate as opportunities arise before you.

16.1 Technique 1: Your Emotions

Many people do not practice the art of self-disciple, so this technique alone will single you out from the rest of the crowd. Whether it be your friends, your co-workers, your clients, or whomever, the ability to become emotionally connected with your goals and your ambitions, the more likely you are to succeed in all aspects of your life.

All leaders are self-discipline and task oriented. Become a leader in your field of interest and take control of your emotions and your life.

Once you decide to take control of your free-will, no one can take this power away from you. Self-discipline begins from within yourself; it is an internal source of human energy, not an external source. The power of human ingenuity develops and grows from within us.

In addition, your environment affects your emotions, but your ability to control yourself, to discipline yourself to conquer obstacles, adapt to minor and major situations, to understand the purpose of mishaps, to welcome hardships, to evaluate your disappointments, is the difference between high performers and average people.

The great thing is, self-discipline is learnable. Anybody can take charge of their own future and destiny—if—they take the time to practice the art of self-discipline and examine their personal and professional life.

Everyone has problems, how you deal with your problems is what will set you apart from the rest of the crowd. Remember, your mind is your greatest asset. If you can control your mind; you can control your life. Control your emotions and discipline yourself to achieve your ambitions.

Increase your personal development and stand out from everyone else. Understand and control why you are thinking what you are thinking, and then, you will open up a new world of opportunities. Take charge of your life, now!

16.2 Technique 2: Your Thoughts

Millions of people do not think about disciplining themselves. But your ability to grasp this key concept will change your life forever. The highest-paid individuals in big organizations are all disciplined in some form or another. They know what they want, what the organization needs, and they do everything in their power to achieve total success at all costs. Over-achievers are disciplined. Politicians are disciplined. All leaders are disciplined. Our laws are disciplined and must be followed.

All constructive and disciplinary actions are first developed in the thought process of the person. Become in sync with your thoughts, examine them, and educate yourself to the fullest.

Continue to discipline yourself every day because not one successful individual in this world has conquered poverty and gained success without practicing the art of self-discipline. The ability to understand and get in touch with your thoughts, your inner-self, and your mind, will help you discipline yourself until it becomes a habit; as a result, you will achieve the success you desire.

How did so many people before us, achieve greatness, self-fulfillment, and prosperity? Their thoughts were set, planned, and disciplined; they only focused on what they wanted and how to get it. Then, they disciplined themselves, they took the time to think about solutions and outcomes, people and places, times and consequences, and took action on their thoughts and ideas.

They were disciplined and resourceful. We must think like successful people do and do what successful people do. Not everything of course, but you get the point. Take what you need, study it, and adjust it to your liking and keep studying the art of self-discipline.

You must decide to become more disciplined and resourceful, so that you may rise, grow, and become a more successful person. Your thoughts, your ideas, and your goals will help you reach and achieve many victories, but discipline is the infinite power that will keep you going and keep you growing.

16.3 Technique 3: Your Decisions

For whatever reason, many people never decide to practice the art of self-discipline. You must dominate and decide to not fall into this category. Decide to change and initiate a road to success. "Everyone wants the good life, but not everybody gets the good life" (Tai Lopez). If you can decide to discipline yourself to read enriching material in your field of interest, you can reach your full potential. If you can go to work and not waste time, you will accomplish more at work and have more time to spend with your family.

Discipline yourself to embrace a great idea and examine it, complete it, and share it with the world. Discipline is the ability to sacrifice time away from your family for a purpose. To discipline yourself and knowing between right and wrong is the key to all successes in life. The ability to self-discipline yourself will ultimately define your future success and recreate massive possibilities and opportunities in your life.

Decide to think about solutions and positive results for your life.

You will be amazed and encouraged at the results when you decide to discipline yourself in all aspects of your life. No matter who you are, what you love to do, and why you want to do it; remember one thing, "Motivation gets you going, but discipline keeps you going and growing." Discipline yourself to get and do what you want in your life, and change your life—forever. You can do this!

16.4 Technique 4: Your Actions

Finally, goals and ambitions are only just that, unless you decide to act upon them, quickly. But if you cannot discipline yourself to remain ambitious, idealistic, and hungry, achieving a more successful life will be more difficult. Your actions will create a tsunami and positive rippling effect, only, if you discipline yourself to take action on all your goals and aspirations in life. Incorporate the art of self-discipline in all aspects of your life: family, business, personal and professional. All leaders are disciplined and goal-oriented.

Every year, all around us, big business and company leaders focus on making money because they are disciplined. Business leaders know the main concept of self-discipline and the principles have not changed for over 200 years, maybe even longer. Gain this philosophy and the main concepts and you will rule your world.

This is why you must understand the consequences of your actions. Discipline is a skill that will help you gain control of your mind, which will help you gain more control of your life. Then, you can gain more control of your goals. Take action and create a keener mindset and become a stronger discipline-oriented person.

Ultimately, you will reach your full potential. Watch as your frame of thinking and your expectations in life—change. Discipline yourself, now and reap the rewards later. Remember, everyone has the same 24 hours in a day, but what you do with that 24 hours, is what will define you and your future success. Take action today and learn the art of self-discipline, today, for greatness exists within you.

16.5 Summary and Execution

1. Master the art of self-discipline and incorporate it into your personal life, your business life, your family life, and anywhere else you desire.

2. You must be strong-minded; you must control your emotions and be able to accept failures. We must fail our way to greatness in order to succeed in life.

3. All political leaders, business leaders, and all leaders, in general, are disciplined. You must become a leader in your field of interest, excel in that field, discipline yourself to study all you need to in that field and conquer it one step at a time.

4. Discipline yourself to know what you want, why you want it, and do everything in your power to get it every single day.

5. The art of self-discipline is learnable, even teachable, so do all you can while you can. Do what is hard now so you can live an easier life later. Most people do what is easy now, but they will live a harder life later. Most people settle for short-term gain and endure long-term pain. You choose!

6. Everyone has problems in life, but it is how you deal with the problems that will separate you from the average person. You will grow at your own pace by practicing the art of self-discipline.

7. Do you currently discipline yourself to do what is necessary every day, if not, why? Reexamine your situation, examine your emotions, your thoughts, your decisions, and your actions: Are the results rewarding or dissatisfying. Know this, self-discipline is the key factor that will fuel your success, help you achieve more goals, reap higher rewards, and succeed with confidence.

CHAPTER 17

Self-Confidence

An Overview

Millions of people around the world may live a confident life, but they do not practice the art of building their own self-confidence on a daily basis. Build a foundation under your life, create a blueprint, and if you are willing, build and strengthen your confidence with every step and action you take in your life. Every action you think about and execute will form a new decision, which will ultimately create a new action with positive or negative results. You make the choice.

Whether you fail or win, the more actions you decide to confront in your life, the faster you gain momentum. You also gain confidence. Our self-esteem rises; our confidence rises; our self-worth increases;

our purpose becomes apparent in our minds; our life begins to engrain success within it, for us, because of us, and undoubtedly, to sustain us with reason and success.

Everyone wants to be successful, but not everyone wants to put in the hard work, and therefore, they will not pursue their dreams. Dream big. Live enormously. Take huge actions on your ideas. Live on purpose and build your confidence in the process. Do not live on the sidelines watching as others pursue their dreams and become successful. "Do not be a follower, be a student of your own personal development" (Jim Rohn).

Follow them, whoever that may be, mimic them if you have to, but take action on your ideas. As you take action on anything you set your mind to, you will build your confidence and feel happier, gain courage, gain the attention of others, and more importantly, be on your way to living a more meaningful and purposeful life.

Reach your full potential and do not let anyone discourage you, for there are many naysayers and doubtful people in this world. Most people resist and never take action on their goals. Do not fall into this category. You are smarter, healthier, and strong-minded. You are powerful. We are powerful. We create our own destinies and successes. Believe in yourself and all your ambitions will become a reality. You can do it!

17.1 Technique 1: Your Emotions

If you can do anything today to help you succeed quicker, change the way you feel when someone disagrees with your ideas. Control your emotions, keep calm, listen to them if you have to, and then move on with your life. Do not live by the standards of others. Build your self-character and feel courageous and strong. In life, your emotional balance is essential and is a determiner to either build your character or crush it to pieces.

Character is who you are, how people see you. If you feel sad, most people will feel sad too. If you feel confident, most people will feel confident. All company leaders are searching for employees who are confident, strong-minded, calm, and can get the assigned task completed with positive results. High-achievers close and seal the deal with poise and confidence and move on to the next prospect. High-performance leaders delegate; they are confident, and they do not let negative situations overcome their future goals for the company.

Are you confident? Are you a leader but just do not know it yet? Ask yourself these questions and explore your inner talents.

If you feel that something is stopping you from performing or feeling your best from within yourself, then change your circumstances. Change your friends, change your surroundings, change who you associate with daily. Someone once said, "You become like the people you associate with and talk to every day." Maybe you need to stop talking to someone, stop going to a certain place, for whatever reason, explore other options and opportunities will form in your life. Discover a more confident you and change your life forever. You can do this!

17.2 Technique 2: Your Thoughts

Millions of people do not worry about their physical appearance, mainly the youth. Experiment with your wardrobe: Study and enhance your vocabulary. If you take the time to think about your fitness, your apparel, and the way you talk to others, you will gain more respect from others. But more importantly, you will increase your self-confidence. You will believe more in yourself. You will have higher and greater expectations for yourself. Before even meeting someone, notice how they perceive you.

The truth is, people see you on the outside before they can even get to know you from the inside. Think of how to make a change, today. What would you change that could impact your future positively? Think about what you can do to change the way people react to you when you walk by them. If you could do anything, what one thing could you do tomorrow that could change your lifestyle and help you build your inner confidence? Only you can make the choice.

The answers to these questions may be simplistic, but the impact can be life-changing. Decide to take charge of your life.

Decide to think about your appearance, your vocabulary, and change your attitude toward all the situations that you confront in life. Can you handle the pressure to change? Change is inevitable. We cannot grow personally and professionally without changing our current situation. All high achievers are self-confident and adaptable to change. All high-performance individuals are confident and have to make big decisions every day for the future of their organizations, respectively.

There are no rules that stop you from becoming a more confident and goal-oriented individual. Believe in yourself, believe you can be a greater person than you already are, believe that you have greatness within you, think positive thoughts daily, think courageously, and with time and much effort, your success will become a reality.

17.3 Technique 3: Your Decisions

Every day, we make decisions that will impact the rest of our day. Within every emotion, there is a thought lingering, with every thought, lies a decision that must be made, and ultimately, an action that must be taken. Your decisions will define your results. But your decisions will also build more confidence because you are dealing with more responsibilities and important actions that must be taken.

How will your decisions help you grow at a personal level? How are your decisions impacting your life—positively or negatively? Evaluate and self-assess yourself to discover your strengths and your weaknesses.

How are your decisions helping you develop personally and professionally? Are your decisions helping you become more confident or weak-minded? Take time to notice what exactly is strengthening you or holding you back from achieving your aspirations and goals in life because with every decision, your confidence grows, or it remains stagnate, or worse, it declines in power.

There is no growth in life without change. So, you must change your decisions if you want to grow your confidence. Every decision has repercussions. So think before you act, but you must act if you want to gain more self-confidence and grow positively, personally, and financially. You can do this!

Your personal development feeds off your minor and major decisions. As your confidence grows, you will be offered bigger responsibilities. Bigger responsibilities mean bigger rewards. Bigger rewards mean bigger opportunities for you to have a more positive impact on your life. The point is, you must gain more confidence in yourself, believe you can do anything you set your mind to do. Gain confidence in yourself and unleash the greatness from within yourself. Take charge of your life and the infinite power that lies from within you. Take action, today!

17.4 Technique 4: Your Actions

Finally, if you will wake up every morning, exercise your mind to think positive thoughts, say positive affirmations, eat healthily, and do something that will help you succeed in your field of interest, you will build more confidence in yourself without a doubt. You will have a mission, your vision for the future will strengthen, and your reason for existing will become stronger and a daily habit for success.

No two people in this world are alike, not even identical twins. You are unique, powerful, and your mind is the key to unlock the potential that lingers within you and the key that will unlock your future success. Take action on what you want, explore how to get it, become more resourceful, and discover the necessary resources you need to help you succeed in all aspects of your life.

Your actions that you take every day will either hinder you from reaching your full potential, or your actions will help you grow your mental state of mind. Earl Nightingale once said long ago, "You become what you think about most of the time." Think in clarity, think with power, and only think about what will help you succeed in life: is it the educational and inspirational books, is it the leaders and people you will meet, is it the seminars, the positive videos, the mentors, and the daily study of yourself—et cetera.

What will help you succeed? Ask yourself and act on that question every day until you discover what or who will truly help you succeed. The goal here is, to build your self-confidence in the process, gain more knowledge, and ultimately, gain more infinite power from within yourself.

Only when you believe in yourself, will you then unlock the doors that will lead you to a more prosperous life of wealth, health, and happiness. Success begins with your personal beliefs. The marvelous thing is, all skills are learnable. Learn how to turn on your confidence when something negative happens. Change your physical and mental state of mind, and build your confidence one action at a time.

If necessary, start in small increments: Build on your major goal. Start to believe in all the opportunities that you have at your disposal in this fast-paced digital age of communication. It is possible! with determination, persistence and self-discipline of the body and the mind. Take action and build the foundation for your future—one incremental steppingstone at a time. You can do this!

17.5 Summary and Execution

1.   The more things and ideas we try in life, regardless if we fail, we build confidence. We are idealistic creatures in nature. Ideally, we want more riches.

2.   Be a student, not a follower. Evaluate yourself. Make it a study to learn all you need to know about yourself: your strengths and your weaknesses. Many big organizations before hiring a person will assess their personality style, their leadership style.

3.   Self-confidence is learnable, teachable, and can be improved over time. Live with a purpose, dream big, and take massive action that can propel you into the future— positively. The more you learn, the more you know, the more you can do. Use It!

4.   Even if you fail, you gain momentum. It is in the process of failing that we succeed in all aspects of our lives. We grow confidently, others grow negatively and worsen their current situation.

5.   Dress for success; your appearance is everything everyone sees on the outside before they get to know you from the inside. Walk and talk like the person you want to become. Study the person you want to be and grow your self-confidence, today!

6.   There is no personal and professional growth in life without change. You must be adaptable. To grow personally and financially, be determined, ambitious, courageous, and confident.

7.   You become just like the people you associate with daily. Who or what is stopping you from growing personally and financially? Is it the people you talk to? Is it your surroundings? What is delaying your future success?

CHAPTER 18

Communication is Vital

―❝―――

Effective communication is 20% what you know and 80% how you feel about what you know.

-Jim Rohn

―――❞―

An Overview

The ability to communicate effectively with others is the key to success. Whether in writing or public speaking, high achievers and high-performance individuals know how to communicate effectively. If they are not experts in the field of communication, then they delegate and hire someone who is.

Every job position in the marketplace began with some form of communication. Whether in a written statement, application, or digital communication, some form of communication is involved in the beginning process of getting any kind of job in any field of interest—across the world.

Your ability to speak and listen, read and write, and communicate what you want in life, is essential in leading you toward a more successful life. The wonderful thing is, all skills are learnable. You can learn how to communicate effectively if you take the time to study and master this vital technique. People in ancient times communicated only by speaking, and eventually, men and women began to write on stones, papyrus, paper, and the list can go on and on.

The point here is, if you can learn to write and speak more clearly, you will communicate more effectively and get what you want in life. Not only will you be able to speak and write more effectively, but you will be able to connect and network with more people across the world. You will also acquire and access more information more readily. You will increase the ability to retain vital information in your field of interest.

Reaching your full potential will be more accessible, feasible, doable and easier for you to fulfill your passions in life. Reach out, take a chance, and learn this skill (the art of communication) and watch and realize as your life changes before you in all aspects of your life. The reward of developing your communication skills is priceless.

18.1 Technique 1: Your Emotions

The majority of people live the rest of their lives without studying the art of reading, writing, speaking and listening. Millions of people do not even make the effort to read a book after graduating from high school. As a result, some people will never again feel the need to grasp the key concepts of communication and why it is important on a personal and professional level.

If you want to become a stronger, smarter, and effective communicator in your field, you must learn to read critically, learn to write effectively, speak with authority and conviction and with clarity, and just as important, we must learn the art of listening. Emotionally, you must understand that there is no greater communication skill more important than reading, writing, speaking and listening. Gain confidence as you study the art of communication and reap the rewards of becoming an effective communicator.

The hard truth is, thinking critically and concisely about what you want in life is a form of communication with one's character. Also, if you can read and write better, you will accomplish more, you will understand more, and you will be more astute in the business world. You will define your purpose in life quicker, smarter, and become more resourceful. You will discover new opportunities, you will discover new people, and you will discover new contacts.

Not to mention, you will feel more confident because you will understand how others communicate in your field of interest. Because of this, you will be able to act more readily, create critical and product results, and in the process, learn the language of your colleagues and their way of communication—if—that is what you are seeking.

Take a chance and take action and feel the impact of world-wide communication at the tips of your fingers with the internet. Take advantage of your resources and unleash the potential that exists within you.

18.2 Technique 2: Your Thoughts

Millions of people do not think about the consequences of their actions when they write or speak on the internet. The truth is, many people do not care what others think. But if you want to grow and become a high achiever, a game-changer, a moneymaker, and become a more successful individual in all aspects of your life, you must think carefully about what you write: personally, publicly, and professionally.

The positive or negative impact of your actions can be life-changing. Someone once said, "We must stand guard at the gate of our mind." Control it, communicate with it, and use your mind to create success, for there is nothing more without communication.

As for your written communication, revise your work, have someone check it for you, find an editor, outsource what you need, anything. But think about the consequences of your written communication before you send it out to the world for others to read. Interpersonal personal communication is a vital foundation of communication that can hurt you or make you into a successful individual, as well as, help you become a stronger leader for your followers, employers, and / or friends and family members. The choice is all yours.

You have the power. You are powerful, you are your greatest asset. Your mind is your greatest asset, so use it to the best of your ability. Gain the fundamental skills of personal and professional communication and reap the rewards. In time, a world of possibilities will open up for you, for your business, or for your enterprise in the making.

Also, whether you are speaking to a small group of people or if you are speaking to millions of people on the internet, plan and practice your speech, prepare your message, study and practice your words. Practice with a friend, practice in front of the mirror, whatever it takes for you to accomplish the thought process and for you to communicate effectively.

Success is possible if you take the time to think about your results—not your activities. Think results, think about solutions when a problem arises. Communication and preparation are essential for all successes in life to be created and become a reality.

Your ability to understand your thoughts, your form of communication, and your vocabulary when you speak, is vital as well. If you plan to reach millions of people throughout the world in a positive way, you must study the art of communication in these four areas: speaking, listening, reading, and writing. It takes practice but it is definitely possible. Do you want to send a positive message? Do you want to gain more attention? Do you want to make more money? What do you want to accomplish in your life?

Whatever your heart desires, if you take the time to communicate your message across many platforms in a positive manner, with conviction, clarity, competence, commitment, and conciseness, you will gain the success you want. Think hard and study past successes in life. Remember, all successful people know how to communicate effectively, and if not, they delegate, and they hire people who read, write, listen, and speak more clearly than they do.

These people relay their messages for them; for example, television networks, radio stations, the internet, politics, all the branches of government, and the list of writers and effective communicators can go on and on. Decide to learn to write and speak more effectively and gain the necessary skills to become a force to be reckoned with in your field of interest. You can do this!

18.3 Technique 3: Your Decisions

If you can decide on anything in your life, decide to invest in yourself. Decide to educate and feed your mind with the necessary skills to communicate in any setting: reading, writing, listening, and speaking are the fundamental skills in any organization. Communicate with one of these skills and you are okay, communicate with two of them, and you will be average, but learn all of these skills and you will shake the world with your message.

Your ability to communicate effectively with others will define your future success. Decide to be aggressive and invest in your personal and professional communication. An educational investment in yourself will not only affect you but millions of others as well—if—that is your mission. You will touch, change, inspire and you will become more valuable to the marketplace in the process of your transformation.

If you decide to learn how to read, write and speak clearer, you have the ability to impact a culture, a society, and possibly—you may impact the world differently. As simple as this skill may sound to you, the ability to use words positively, can move mountains, start a civil war, or start a new revolution.

Whatever your cause, whatever you need, for whatever reason, whatever your goals are, decide to learn the necessary skills to communicate more effectively and observe as your life changes and opportunities arise before you. You will not regret the moment, the time, the effort, the courage, and the discipline that it takes to learn the necessary skills to become more successful in life. Invest in your future, now, for yesterday is history.

18.4 Technique 4: Your Actions

Finally, the ability to feel, think, decide, and take action is all that is left on your agenda. It has been stated before, "without action there is no success in life." You must rise, learn, and be all that you can be. Reach your full potential and impact the lives of others by simply communicating more effectively and you can get what you want in life. If you fail, try again.

Les Brown once said, "Not everyone can say no to you, eventually, someone will say yes." There is much truth in this statement. There is hope for success as long as there is a heartbeat in your chest. How much do you want to succeed? How much time are you willing to sacrifice for the future of your success? How much more communication skills do you need to take you to the next level of your success? How many books do you have to read? How many seminars do you have to attend or watch online? Keep asking yourself, "What actions do I have to take to gain financial freedom?"

You have to stay hungry and want more out of life. Become an effective communicator by taking action, today. Everyone deserves to be respected; everybody wants the good life, but not everyone gets what they want in life. It has been said, "If you want respect, you have to earn it."

Do not underestimate the power of the written word. Seek opportunities and you shall find answers. Remember, leaders, are readers. Leaders are writers. Leaders are great listeners. Leaders speak with conviction and passion, some more than others. But the point here is, high achievers are confident, educated, and know how to communicate effectively with their intended audience. Become a student, take action in your life, and communicate effectively and with a purpose. Learn the art of communication.

Invest in yourself. Self-teach yourself if you have to. If you invest in yourself, now, you will reap the rewards for the rest of your life. The days, weeks, and months are going to pass anyways, so you might as well do your best to gain the success you desire, the future you want, and the communication skills that can transform your life.

18.5 Summary and Execution

1. The art of communication consists of four basic concepts and skills: reading, writing, listening, and speaking. Learn and use a couple of these skills, you will be average. But, study, learn, and use all four of them, and you will shake the world.

2. The ability to communicate with others in your field of interest is essential. Learn their language, learn their vocabulary, and learn their philosophy and communicate accordingly.

3. We all communicate every day. How will you choose to communicate? Think about the consequences of your communication beforehand.

4. Invest in yourself, invest in your personal development. Learn the fundamental skills in communication that can shake the world. Study it!

5. Do you want to send a positive message? Do you want to gain more attention? Do you want to make more money? What do you want to accomplish in your life? Either way, communication is involved.

6. Civilization has invented, created wealth, survived through wars, and flourished through the agricultural age, the industrial age, the information and services age, and right now, we are capitalizing and living in the communications age. Take advantage of all the resources that are available.

7. Remember, leaders are readers, writers, great listeners, speak with conviction, passion, and know how to communicate effectively with their intended audience. You must study the art of communication and create your own communication style.

CHAPTER 19

Time Management

An Overview

Every person has the same 24 hours. The ability to use your time wisely is the most powerful strategy to becoming more productive, getting more done, and ultimately, becoming more successful in all aspects of your life. You can spend money and get more money again, but you cannot waste time and get it back. You must be careful and pay close attention to what is taking up so much of your time in your life. Remember, time is our most valuable asset.

Is something or someone holding you back from completing and fulfilling your goals and dreams? If so, identify the situation, identify a solution, implement it, and plan accordingly. You must allocate the necessary time for what is important in your life: your planned-out goals, your family, and your financial freedom agenda.

What do you want to accomplish right now? What is more valuable in your life right now? What areas in your life need more of your time and attention? What matters need less of your time? Identify them and plan accordingly. Do you not have enough time to achieve success and reach your full potential? Why? Ask yourself these questions and discover the situations that are holding you back, hindering you, and slowing you down from succeeding.

Identify the reasons, isolate the problem, change the activity or the outcome, and make the necessary time you need to do what is necessary. Take the time to examine your life and you will change your life forever.

19.1 Technique 1: Your Emotions

Become a time management expert and use the time to your advantage. Calculate the 24 hours in your daily, weekly, and monthly schedule and plan accordingly. If you know how your time is being used, you will identify why you need more time and in what areas you need it more or less. This technique alone will help you define your future success.

Once you can understand why you need more time in your life. Only you can accomplish more meaningful goals for yourself. If you will allocate your time accordingly, your aspirations will become a reality. Not to mention, you will respect and be grateful for the time you have on this Earth. You will not waste one minute of your life on what is not important or waste time on what is not helping you reach your full potential. Remember, time is vital and a valuable resource amongst others, but indefinitely, time rules our lives. So, we must be careful about how we use our 24 hours every day.

Many people do not feel as if their time is important, some do not care. Most people are not aware of the skill and the concept of time management. Time management is a marvelous skill to have in your arsenal, and it is learnable. You can master the art of time management.

If your emotions drive you to want more out of life, then seek more opportunities. You deserve more, so take the time to appreciate life more. But more importantly, cherish, be grateful, and use your time wisely to get more of what you want in your life. You can do this!

19.2 Technique 2: Your Thoughts

The ability to discipline yourself to think about what you must do even when you do not want to do it, is the hardest thing that many people fail to accomplish and overcome. If you want to be more successful, you have to accomplish more things in life. So think about what you need to do every day to get you closer to achieving your primary goal, and from the time you wake up, to the time you go to sleep, use your time effectively. Think about success all the time.

Take the time to schedule your days, your weeks, your months, and the years ahead of you if you can. Make a plan for your future and wonderful rewards will follow your actions. Your thoughts are the predictor of your future success. Think excellence all the time; think opportunities; think of your goals; think about why you want to succeed, and think positively all the time. Learn to control your thoughts and emotions simultaneously.

All high achievers, successful business leaders, and entrepreneurs schedule their days in minutes and hours. They understand the value of time. In most cases, they have secretaries to schedule their agendas. This technique: prioritizing your time and how it is used every day, can help you accomplish more in the next six months than most people will accomplish in a lifetime.

Your frame of thinking about what is important in your life is the key to your success. Value your time, make time for what is important in your life, and gain the attention of your superiors in the process. You will reap the benefits of being a strategic planner of time—your time; your life; your future; your goals. What are you waiting for? Unleash your full potential, today!

Remember, once you think hard about what it is that is stopping you and holding you back from accomplishing your goals, only then, will you will identify the problem, extinguish it, and push it out of your life. You must make better judgments on how to use your time; your time will be more meaningful, and you will gain more satisfaction, more happiness, and self-fulfillment out of your life.

Ultimately, you will have more strategic time to progress: mentally, physically, and financially because you will spend more of your time chasing your goals, completing your goals, and discovering new goals in the process. As a result, more opportunities and more important people will arise in your life. Decide to use your time wisely and change your life forever.

19.3 Technique 3: Your Decisions

Decide to become an expert time manager of your life. Decide to discipline yourself to know who, what, where, and when to use your time effectively. No other skill is more important and correlates and separates the average individual from the highly driven successful individual. You can become an expert time manager, only, if you have the desire to change the way you use your time on a daily basis. You can do this!

Remember, time equals money, and your time equals life. Time is a fundamental skill in life management. Time is the fundamental resource that we must not take for granted. If you decide to organize your time, you are patterning your life for success. Decide to achieve success. Decide to allocate your time positively and efficiently and you will become the best person you are meant to be.

Decide to eliminate time wasters in your life. Decide to schedule your appointments in a calendar or in a daily planner or both. If you are willing, make a list of everything that has to be done by a certain time on a certain day. If you have to make phone calls, call everyone in an orderly fashion, eliminate all your calls in one day—in the order of importance; prioritize as needed.

If you decide to manage your activities, you can manage the outcome of your goals. Also, you will gain a higher sense of satisfaction, authority, and self-fulfillment when you take charge of your time, your life, and ultimately, your future success. You will begin to see patterns and daily routines will become a habit. The habits eventually will become automatic. The benefits of controlling and itemizing your time, will reward you in abundance.

For example, you will have more time with your family if that is what you seek. You will have more time for yourself if that is what you want. You will have more time with prospects if that is what you need. You will have more time for the foreseeable future if that is what you desire.

Decide to become an expert time manager and you will accomplish more in the next year than most people will accomplish in a lifetime. Take action: plan, schedule, respect your time, cherish the minutes and the hours of the day, and prioritize your time, today!

19.4 Technique 4: Your Actions

Finally, your actions will define your success. So, implement, dominate, and prioritize your time accordingly. The ability to use your time to your advantage, first, and not to the advantage of others, will define your successes in life. You must be selfish in a sense.

If you will learn to become a time manager in your life, you will inevitably attract opportunities into life. You will be paid more. You will be respected more. You will become more influential. You will be an example to others. The list and benefits can go on and on.

But the point here is, time management is an essential skill to learn and like all skills, time management is learnable. You must master the ability to control your time in your own life, if not, someone will always be there to control it for you. If you decide to anything, today, take action and identify where the majority of your time is being used and by whom.

With all sincerity, understand that we all have the same 24 hours in one day. But what you do with your time, will either impact your future success—negatively or positively. In the end, we all have 24 hours in a day to use and yes, we all have problems to deal with, too, but it is how we deal with our problems that define us.

Do you allow your problems to hinder you from achieving success; instead, learn from them, use them, and examine them but not for too long. Knowing how to overcome adversities and move forward, will ultimately define you. You are strong. You are capable. You are alive and well, and your time is precious on this Earth. Use your time with precision, purpose, dignity, and integrity.

Your time should not be taken for granted. Use it, do not abuse it, for time is the essential, the powerful, and the almighty, life-fulfilling key factor that will ultimately define your future success. Take action, today! And take your success to the next level by prioritizing your time, today! You can do this!

19.5 Summary and Execution

1. Every person has the same 24 hours. The ability to use your time wisely is the most powerful strategy to becoming more productive, getting more done, and ultimately, becoming more successful.

2. Is something or someone holding you back from completing and fulfilling your goals and dreams? If so, you must allocate the necessary time for what is important in your life: your planned-out goals, your family, and your financial freedom agenda.

3. Calculate the 24 hours in your daily, weekly, and monthly schedule and plan accordingly. If you know how your time is being used, you will be able to plan better, achieve more goals, and succeed.

4. All high achievers, successful business leaders, and entrepreneurs schedule their days in minutes and hours. They understand the value of time. You must do the same. Become and time-management expert.

5. You will have more time with your family, for yourself, for prospects, and for your goals if that is what you seek. Decide to become an expert time manager and you will accomplish more in the next year than most people will accomplish in a lifetime.

6. Implement, dominate, and prioritize your time accordingly. The ability to use your time to your advantage, first, and not to the advantage of others, will define your successes in life. Remember: time = money.

7. With all sincerity, understand that we all have the same 24 hours in one day. But what you do with your time, will either impact your future success negatively or positively.

CHAPTER 20

Personal Development

An Overview

The majority of people are introduced, attend, and learn the curricula from a public education. Most people will learn theoretically in elementary school, junior high school, and high school. Even college introduces knowledge to you, but not how to use the knowledge to better yourself, your future, and your financial situations in life. To increase your chances of success, you must begin to develop yourself—mentally and physically. Continue to grow and learn all you need to know to become a highly successful individual.

Invest the necessary time to develop yourself, so that you may have the opportunity to reach your full potential. Spend more time reading more knowledgeable books, developing your personal skills and conditioning your mind. It has been said, "Knowledge is power," but the truth is, "Knowledge is only potential power," until you learn how to use it and master *The Art of Personal Development*.

All high achievers, all high performers, all entrepreneurs, all business leaders from various fields and industries, in some form or way, have studied and mastered the ability to develop themselves on a personal level. You too must understand the importance of dedicating each and every day to enhancing your mind and body. Condition your mind for excellence so that you may excel in your field of interest. You can do this!

Do not be overwhelmed or discouraged. The ability to better yourself and get what you want out of life begins with your personal development. Take charge of your life. Take the time and invest in your future by simply investing in yourself. Take full responsibility for your actions and develop—and take in new knowledge intentionally. Only you can make this change. Only you have the power to change your life. Only you can impact the world in a way that no one else can. Only you!

20.1 Technique 1: Your Emotions

Millions of people fail to further develop themselves on a personal level. Why? I do not know why. But, you must not be placed in this category of undeveloped self-potential. Explore your full potential and discover more opportunities in the process.

You must oversee your future success, develop your feelings, strengthen your emotions, and pursue your dreams and goals in life. Follow your gut feeling. Follow your passion. Follow your ideas and reach your full potential. Becoming self-aware of your emotions and identifying your strengths, is a wonderful skill to acquire.

Your personal development is charged by your emotional mindset. If you can control your emotions, you can control your thoughts, if you can control your thoughts, you can control your decisions, and ultimately, you can control your actions. As a result, your actions will define your future success in the form of positive outcomes. Succeed intentionally not accidentally.

If you can exercise your mind and not only your body, you will gain more success in life. You will trigger the law of attraction. Emotionally, you will gain confidence; you will focus on your personal skills more; you will eat healthier, and you will begin your journey toward a more successful future.

You want more out of your life because you deserve more. Change the way you feel, and you will change the way you think about success. Only then, will positive thoughts and positive people begin to enter your life more rapidly, deliberately, and automatically.

20.2 Technique 2: Your Thoughts

The more you think about success, the more you will want it. Logically, the newer information you learn, study, and review, the more you absorb and understand how others around you became successful. Remember, success leaves clues.

Remain optimistic, think only positive thoughts about how to change your current situation if that is what you desire. Change the way you live, talk, walk, work and think. Only then, will you acquire, obtain, and reach your full potential in life if this is what you seek.

Someone once said, "No one has ever discovered the limit of human potential." We can learn as much as we push our minds to take in, as much as we believe to be enough. How much knowledge is enough for you? How much further are you willing to push yourself to learn all you need to know to increase your personal development. Your personal philosophy will define your future success. Simply think about what you want and how you are going to get it.

The law of attraction is simple. The more you think about developing yourself in a positive manner, the more you will be introduced to different people, different opportunities, and even, different avenues of income.

If you are willing, use your mind to your advantage and think, grow, and develop a rich and fulfilling mind-set. When you learn *The Art of Personal Development*, only then, will you cherish and be grateful for every minute of the day, for every idea in the day, for every person you meet in the day, for every situation that you encounter in the day, and for every night that follows the day.

Keep a journal and record your life if possible, do not let your mind become a file cabinet. Save the most valuable moments in your life; reflect on them, use them, study them, and review them. It has been stated many times, "Repetition is the mother of all skill." Become a student and learn all you need to know to help you reach financial freedom, hey, the time is going to pass anyways. We might as well take advantage of the time we have on this Earth.

Take advantage of our resources and empower ourselves, develop ourselves, and capitalize on every situation, is the ultimate goal in life.

Eventually, the more your work on your personal development, the more you will think about the consequences and the importance of how to use your time effectively to advance your current situation—in all aspects of your life. Decide to develop your personal skills, today!

20.3 Technique 3: Your Decisions

Everyone makes decisions in life. However, not every decision has the same outcome nor the same effect. What will you decide to change in your life tomorrow? Will it change your life forever? Will you remain an average individual or will self-develop yourself into a new person that will create new and bountiful opportunities? Make the critical choice and the right choice to personally develop yourself. You deserve to be successful. You owe it to yourself to at least try. You will be amazed at the outcomes.

Recreate your life and take ahold of your destiny. Your decision to refine a particular skill is essential. You need to improve every day. You need to decide whether you want to better your current situation, enhance it, or completely redefine your life's personal plan—if you have one. If not, create one. Become a leader, a strategic thinker, and decide to envision your success; it is possible!

Do you want to remain on a plateau, or do you want to live on an upward incline, continuously increasing your life's potential?

Only by raising the stakes, by taking a risk, by raising your expectations and living to the fullest, only then, will you personally develop yourself intentionally, and in the process—develop a more prosperous and happy life for you, but more importantly, for the future of your family.

How bad do you want success? How bad do you want to become financially self-sufficient? Are you willing to sacrifice friends, family, and your time? Decide and take action on your goals, today. You can do this!

20.4 Technique 4: Your Actions

Finally, your actions will define your success. If anything is more important in life, more eminent, more powerful, more life-changing, more spontaneous—it is the ability to take action on your next endeavors in becoming a highly successful and driven individual. Take action, today and succeed, today!

The ability to self-discipline yourself to become a positive, rich-thinking, and action-oriented individual—will ultimately separate you from the average person. Take action and take charge of your life. Take the time to act and refine your personal skills; redefine your purpose in life; refine your mentality, and master *The Art of Personal Development*.

Never blame others for your failures. Taking full responsibility for your actions is a sign of maturity and a leadership quality. Never blame the government. Never blame family members, never blame the economy or anyone else for that matter. When you realize that no one but yourself is to blame, only then, will you be able to focus on the positive and the beautiful things in life. You are the most important person in your life.

It is not what happens in life that will determine your future; instead, it is what you do, what you read, what you study, what you watch, what information you take in, and what you think about most of the time, this is what will ultimately lead you to the better things in life that you want, need, and seek.

Overall, if you can take action on anything in life, change yourself from the inside out. You cannot change the external situations in your life, but you can change the internal situations in your life. You may not be able to change the destination in your life in one day, but you can change the direction in which you want to continue; in the end, it is your choice.

Remember, you are the most important person in the world. Take charge of your life and become a personal development expert. Remember, every skill is learnable.

Self-develop yourself and take action and carefully watch as your life, your opportunities, and your goals begin to unravel and attract more potential prospects. Take action, today!

20.5 Summary and Execution

1. To increase your chances of success, you must begin to develop yourself mentally and physically. Continue to grow and learn all you need to know to become a highly successful individual.
2. Understand the importance of dedicating every day to nourishing your mind and body. Condition your mind; reprogram it, and control it.
3. Foresee your future success, develop your feelings, strengthen your emotions, pursue your dreams and goals in life. Reach your full potential.
4. If you can control your emotions, you can control your thoughts, if you can control your thoughts, you can control your decisions, and ultimately, you can control your actions. As a result, your actions will define your future success in the form of positive outcomes. Succeed intentionally, not accidentally.
5. The more you think about success, the more you will want it. Logically, the newer information you learn, study, and review, the more you absorb and understand how others around you became and are becoming more successful. Remember, success leaves clues.
6. Recreate your life and take ahold of your destiny. Your decision to refine a particular skill is essential. You need to improve every day. You need to decide whether you want to better your current situation, enhance it, or completely redefine your life's personal plan—if you have one. If not, create one.
7. Take the time to act and refine your personal skills; redefine your purpose in life; refine your mentality, and master *The Art of Personal Development*. The ability to self-discipline yourself to become a positive, rich-thinking, and action-oriented individual—will ultimately separate you from the average person.

CHAPTER 21

Find a Mentor

An Overview

A person pursuing his or her ambitions without a mentor or a coach, is a person not being pushed to reach their full potential in life. A mentor is critical to your future plan toward living and achieving a more blissful life. A mentor can help you see things you thought were not even possible. A coach can push you to achieve greatness in any particular aspect of your life: business, fitness, schooling, and personal development, just to name a few.

If you want to gain more intelligence and success faster; you need to find someone that can help you achieve greatness. A mentor will help you manage your time, your money, and ultimately, a mentor will help you focus your mental powers so that you can use every atom of energy in your body to maximize your full potential.

Also, with access to the worldwide net, we have the ability to learn more from others. Observe how other successful people have grown personally and financially. All major successful people have had coaches at some point in their lives.

For example, remember the Olympians, the athletes, Hollywood actors, schoolteachers, college and university instructors and professors, business leaders, politicians, and even the president of the United States of America—have had some form of guidance, instruction, coaching, advising, and personal assistance to reach and take advantage of their full potential.

You may succeed in life gradually, but a mentor will help you conquer life's challenges efficiently and quickly. Take the time to listen to someone who can help you be more successful in all aspects of your life, whether by video, webinar, seminar, in-person, or by whatever other means of media.

21.1 Technique 1: Your Emotions

Most people drift through life without any guidance. A mentor can help you gain the self-confidence to pursue your dreams and achieve your goals. A coach can help you grow your self-esteem, become smarter, become more flexible, become more confident, and ultimately, help you succeed and achieve your specific goals.

Emotionally, you can do anything you set your mind to do, but you must gain this emotional intelligence first. Become self-aware of your emotions and of the emotions of those around you, specifically your followers or of those you wish to study and learn from them.

Do you want to know what you can do to enhance your personal skills? Do you want to erase the negative emotional feelings that cloud your judgments? Do you want to single out your goals: physically, mentally, and emotionally? Do you want to succeed?

Do you want more out of life? Do you want to reach your full potential? Well, the wonderful thing is, there is a coach for just about everything that you desire. We have the necessary resources for success, but we must search and seek guidance, experience, and the knowledge that will propel us to the next level of achievement.

Remember, there is an individual coach for every particular field of interest: business, life, financial success, personal development, fitness, and the list can go on and on. Metaphorically speaking, you must sharpen your skill—the #1 skill that will help you rise out of obscurity and become financially self-sufficient and work on that skill every day—every day until you succeed. Repeat this process, for repetition, is the mother of all skill.

From an emotional standpoint, a mentor will help you develop mentally. You can learn to control your negative emotions as well as use your positive emotions to take your success to the next level quicker.

A mentor will help you learn to express and study your positive emotions in a way you never thought of. In the end, every person has greatness within them. Find a mentor and raise your expectations, take your emotions and your success to the next level of greatness.

21.2 Technique 2: Your Thoughts

Many people think they can live a prosperous life without any guidance, but that is a lie. Everyone needs someone. When you were a child, you needed your parents. You looked up to them. As you grew, you looked up to your friends and your environment. As the years passed, your schoolteachers became your mentors. A mentor may be all that you need to take your success ambitions to the next level.

Nonetheless, understand and think hard, with age and time, thereafter, comes knowledge, but with knowledge comes responsibility, and with responsibility, comes power.

Many of us go through life with so much unused power within us. Which side of the spectrum do you think you are on? Your ability to think about the importance of a mentor can change your life forever.

A mentor will not only change your life, but he or she will also engrain positive thoughts and scenarios for you to rise from an average person: to a mentally, physically, thoughtful, and powerful person. Decide to experience the difference that a mentor can make in your life toward achieving your goals, today, tomorrow, and forever.

21.3 Technique 3: Your Decisions

If there is anything you can do to increase more productivity out of yourself, it is following the guidance, the decisions, of a mentor. The outcomes of having a mentor will astonish you. Your life will change instantaneously. Your emotions will change instantly. Your thoughts will become purposeful. Your decisions will be more meaningful, and your actions will perform wonders that you thought were never possible.

Decide to find a mentor. A colleague, a trustworthy and smart individual that has only your positive perspectives in mind. A mentor is only interested in one thing: to educate you, your personal development and/or a specific area of your choice, striving to enhance and raise your expectations. Remember, a mentor can help you develop your personal skills and your knowledge, which is essential in bettering yourself; mentally, physically, and financially.

If you will decide to discover mentors in all aspects of your life, you will open up a portal to more positive opportunities, different avenues and paths for success, and ultimately, the possibility for financial connections—worldwide. Take action, today!

21.4 Technique 4: Your Actions

Finally, your ability to identify the importance of a mentor and taking action on that concept, can change your life forever. Your actions will be more concise, more exact, more meaningful, more important and more aggressive. In this marketplace, we need mentors to study, to listen to, and we need to follow the teachings of a personal coach; as a result, we will grow and gain more self-confidence in ourselves.

The fact is, he or she can help you fulfill your short-term and long-term goals, and you will accomplish and get more out of your life as you attempt to work on your personal development.

Follow by example; remember, success leaves clues. All successful people took action by means of coaching. All successful individuals developed themselves, first. All successful people never gave up on their dreams and goals. All successful individuals went out into the world and failed, first, but prevailed in the end.

The desire to succeed in life regardless of what anyone thought about them was not on their mind at the time, but they took action by all means necessary.

All successful individuals have fought and conquered. They tried and succeeded. They fell and got back up. All successes in life have failed before they prevailed and triumphed. The number one thing that all these successes and successful people have in common is, they all had someone in their corner, maybe a support system, a friend, or a mentor.

The boxer had a coach in his ear. The basketball player had a coach breathing down his neck. The football player had a coach yelling in his face. The business leader and CEO of a company had an advisor on his back at all times. The list can go on and on. Woman or man, it is possible to succeed in this life, but a mentor can help you get there quicker.

The point here is, no one ever got successful in life alone. If you want to rise in your field, take action, today. Some mentors are already long and gone, but they have written or recorded how they became successful. Learn from their failures and successes. Learn from their obstacles and mishaps.

Someone once said, "Do not reinvent the wheel," for everything you need is around you. You just might need someone to guide you to it, and a mentor can help you find it.

Take action and read the books in your field of interest. Focus on one skill that will help you achieve success: Listen to powerful seminars; listen to purposeful webinars, go to professional conferences and meaningful forums and business gatherings that coincide with your interest. The more you search, the more you will find. "The more you learn, the more you will earn." Find a mentor and change your life—forever. Who knows, in the end, you may become a positive and powerful mentor.

21.5 Summary and Execution

1. A mentor is critical for living and achieving your major goals. A mentor can help you see things you thought were not even possible, can push you to achieve greatness in a particular area like business, fitness, schooling, and your personal development.

2. If you want to gain more intelligence and success faster; you need to find a mentor that will help you manage your time, your money, and every atom of energy in your body to reach its full potential.

3. You may succeed in life gradually, but a mentor will help you conquer life's challenges efficiently and quickly. Take the time to listen to someone who can help you, whether by video, webinar, seminar, in-person, or by whatever other means of media.

4. Remember, there is an individual coach for every particular field of interest. Sharpen your skill—the #1 skill that will help you rise out of obscurity and become financially self-sufficient and work on that skill every day—every day until you succeed.

5. A mentor will not only change your life, but he or she will also engrain positive thoughts and scenarios for you to rise from an average person, to a mentally, physically fit and powerful person.

6. The outcomes of having a mentor will astonish you. Your life will change instantaneously. Your emotions, thoughts, decisions, and actions will change instantly.

7. The point here is, no one ever got successful in life alone. If you want to rise in your field, take action, today. Some mentors are already long and gone, but they have written or recorded how they became successful. Learn from their failures and successes.

ABOUT
THE AUTHOR

J.R. Fitzgerald is a writer and mentor who has found solace and serenity in writing both fiction and non-fiction since 2013. He gained momentum in his writing career after realizing that his rhyming words and poetic language intrigued both his high school classmates and instructors.

Associations:

He is a Member of "The National Society of Leadership and Success." He also tutors youngsters in his community and at the Universities.

J.R. was born in Houston, Texas to immigrant parents from Monterrey, Nuevo Leon, Mexico, and graduated from Lone Star College with a Liberal Arts Associate's Degree. He holds a Bachelor of Science Degree in Technical Communication from the University of Houston.

Awards:

In 2016, he won the "Lone Star College Foundation Essay Scholarship Award." In 2019, he earned the "Certificate of Leadership and Excellence Award" followed by the "Advanced Leadership Certification" in 2020.

Interests:

In addition to writing, J.R. loves to plant trees, draw, sketch and paint, work on car engines, cook delicious cuisines and spend time with family and friends. His life's ambition is to assist others to discover and develop their full potential. He is passionate about helping others to realize that they are powerful, smart, and that their mind is their greatest asset. He plans to author more books, including collections for children, but more importantly, continue to help people of all ages *Develop A Genius Mindset* so they too can unleash their full potential and achieve unimaginable success.

INDEX

THANK YOU

Thank you for purchasing this book and the interest to *Develop A Genius Mindset*. I hope after reading and practicing every principle that benefits you, you will be inspired, motivated, or directed and instructed and a step closer toward reaching your full potential.

Next to our family, there is nothing more important in this world than self-education. I would like to praise you for taking the time to invest in your personal development. In all honesty, if you have not already, if you will do what is hard now; I truly do believe you can *Unleash Your Full Potential And Achieve Unimaginable Success* in all aspects of your life.

Humbly, I would also like to ask you to please leave a review at your earliest convenience. Your comments and/or questions will not only help me identify what you enjoyed or disapproved of but how to better structure my next writing projects. Thank you for your time and may all your thoughts come into focus.

Sincerely and Yours Truly,

-J.R. Fitzgerald